THE
BLACK
HERITAGE
BOOK OF
TRIVIA

by Morgan White, Jr.

Cover design by Tina Chomka

Library of Congress Catalog Card Number
84-63110
ISBN 0-9611268-9-2

First printing September 1985
Second printing October 1985

Photographs courtesy of:

Chicago Mayor's Office (p. 95)
Edward Brooke (p. 97)
Los Angeles Mayor's Office (p. 99)
Aaron Spelling Productions (p. 102)
Atlanta Mayor's Office (p. 103)
Boston Celtics (p. 105)
Boston Red Sox (p. 106)
Warner Brothers Films (pp. 96, 98, 100, 101, 104)

DEDICATION

To Jean, Mary, Sharon and Evan—my family.

Special thanks to Neil Midman, without whose help I could not have finished this book within its deadline.

Table of Contents

QUESTIONS

HISTORY

1. Who was the first black born in the English colonies (Jamestown, Virginia)?

2. In 1704, who opened a school in New York City for black slaves?

3. Who was the first bishop of the African Methodist Episcopal Zion Church?

4. What was the name of the first Negro newspaper?

5. Who was Oliver Cromwell?

6. Absalom Jones and Richard Allen were the founders of what organization?

7. Where and when was the first Negro Masonic Lodge in America organized?

8. Where and when was the organization of the African Methodist Church?

9. Where was the first Negro Episcopal congregation located in the US?

10. What was the name of the first Negro periodical?

11. Who was the first black to be admitted to the bar in the US?

12. Who formed the Underground Railroad?

13. Who was the first American Negro Roman Catholic bishop?

14. Who was the first black to be admitted to practice before the Supreme Court?

15. Who was the first black woman to graduate from Howard University Law School?

16. Who was the first black to preside over a national political gathering?

17. Where was the first training school for black nurses in the US?

18. Where and when was the founding of the National Negro Business League?

19. Where and when was the NAACP founded?

20. Who founded the National Council of Negro Women?

21. Who was the first black woman judge in the US?

22. What year was the Civil Rights Act passed?

23. What was the first Negro land grant college?

24. Who was the first black general of the US Army?

25. What organization did Martin Luther King, Jr. represent when he delivered his famous "I Have a Dream" speech?

26. In what year was Adam Clayton Powell, Jr. elected to Congress?

27. Which amendment abolished slavery, and in what year was it passed?

28. Where and in what year was the American Negro Academy founded?

29. Who was the first black principal in New York City?

30. The railway telegraph, the electric railway system and the steam boiler furnace were all invented by one man. Name him.

31. What is the oldest black religious denomination in the US?

32. Who was the first black person honored on a postage stamp?

33. What do the **Bronze Raven**, the **Oklahoma Eagle**, **The Lighthouse** and **The Outlook** all have in common?

34. John Scobell was a spy for the Union Army during the Civil War. Name the famous detective agency that trained him.

35. Who was the first black woman to be admitted to the Mississippi bar?

36. Who was Fannie Lou Hamer?

37. Who was the first black woman to be Assistant US Attorney?

38. Who was the first black to represent the US at the United Nations?

39. The first black slaves were brought to what state in the English colonies in America, and in what year?

40. Marcus Garvey organized the first Black mass movement. What was it called?

41. The black man's right to vote was guaranteed by which amendment?

42. Who was the first black person to earn a Ph.D. at Harvard?

43. What was originally known as the "Niagara Movement"?

44. What was the name of the squadron led by Colonel Benjamin Davis?

45. What was known as "Black Monday"?

46. What was the occupation of Pedro Alonzo Nino?

47. Who was Jean Baptiste Point?

48. Who was the first black medical doctor in America?

49. Who were Peter Salem and Salem Poor?

50. The first law against slavery was passed in what year?

51. Who was John Russwurm?

52. When did blacks become full citizens of the US?

53. Hiram Revels and Blanche K. Bruce were senators from which state?

54. Who was the founder of the Tuskegee Institute?

55. Who was the founder of the newspaper, **The Chicago Defender**?

56. Who were Henry Johnson and Needham Roberts?

57. Who was Crispus Attucks?

58. Who won the Nobel Peace Prize in 1964?

59. Who was the first black to give a recital in Symphony Hall in Boston?

60. Who was the first black to conduct a major American orchestra?

61. On what occasion was the NAACP founded?

62. In what year was the National Urban League founded?

63. Where and in what year did Jesse Owens win his four gold Olympic medals?

64. Who was Undersecretary to the United Nations in 1951?

65. In what year did Eli Whitney patent the cotton gin?

66. Where was the first black college located?

67. One of the most famous court cases during the 1930s was the rape trial involving the Scottsboro Boys. In what state did this take place?

68. Abraham Pierce was the only black American to be part of what well-known group?

69. Sojourner Truth, famed speaker against slavery, changed her name in 1843. What was her original first name?

70. The decision of **Plessie** v. **Ferguson** was overturned by what 1950 court case?

71. What did the Missouri Compromise prohibit?

72. The first Civil Rights Act, giving equal rights to blacks in 1875, was invalidated by the Supreme Court in what year?

73. In 1831, William Lloyd Garrison created a newspaper dedicated to abolitionism. Name his paper.

74. In 1831 in Virginia, one of the biggest slave revolts in American history took

place. Name the fearless slave who led this uprising.

75. What was the nickname runaway slaves gave to Harriet Tubman?

76. Toussaint L'Ouverture successfully forced all French, British and Spanish soldiers off of his homeland in Haiti in the early 1800s. He freed all of the slaves on the island and remained their leader until, in an effort to bring a halt to continued fighting, he accepted the words of peace from a European ruler. Once the fighting ended, this ruler had Toussaint thrown in jail, where the ex-slave soon died a lonely death. Name the ruler who betrayed him.

77. In what year did Dr. Ralph Bunche win the Nobel Peace Prize?

78. Where was the Hampton Institute, the first school for free blacks (circa 1861) located?

79. Name the two track stars who held their fists high in a black power salute during the 1968 Olympics.

80. Amherst College has named one of its student quarters after the man who perfected the technique of blood transfusion. Name him.

81. The next time you are panicking because you are going to be late, you can probably blame Garrett Morgan, as one of his inventions might be holding you up. What is it?

82. The late Dr. Carter Woodson began calling the second week in February "Black History Week" in 1926. Why?

83. Who began the "Black Star Line," the first all-black shipping company?

84. Louis Lattimer assisted with some of the most important innovations in sound technology early this century; although his boss usually gets the credit, Lattimer himself improved or perfected a number of his boss' inventions. Name his boss.

85. What country introduced slavery to the US?

86. As well as being a great inventor, Benjamin Banneker helped to plan the layout of one of America's most important cities. Name the city.

87. Henry Flipper was the first black to graduate from this Eastern-based school in 1877. Name it.

88. What cargo would most ships pick up after unloading slaves in America?

89. If you saw someone wearing a green ribbon a few years ago, what would it symbolize?

90. Harry Truman is credited with desegregating the Armed Forces. What man was instrumental in supplying the president with information towards that end?

91. Robert Gould Shaw was a Union officer in the Civil War. What was unique about his command?

92. To what branch of the Armed Services did writer Alex Haley belong?

93. Mary M. Bethune began one of the most used phrases in black culture since the mid-'60s. What phrase is it?

94. Name the black performer who lost his popular TV variety series after less than a season because sponsors were afraid of whites boycotting their products.

95. During the decade of the '70s, what American had the "most recognized face in the world"?

96. Name the famous jazz singer who bled to death because an all-white hospital near where she had a car accident would not admit her.

LITERATURE

1. Who wrote **To Be Young, Gifted and Black** (1968)?

2. Oscar Micheaux's first film was an adaptation of his novel. Name the film.

3. For what was James Weldon Johnson noted?

4. Who was Phyllis Wheatley?

5. What was the first play by black playwright Lorraine Hansberry to win the New York Drama Critics Award as Best Play?

6. Who was the first black to be awarded the Pulitzer Prize for Poetry?

7. Who wrote the novels **Drums at Dusk** and **Black Thunder**?

8. Whose autobiography was entitled **Black Boy**?

9. Who wrote **The Living Is Easy**?

10. Who wrote the 1953 novel **Go Tell It on the Mountain**?

11. **Jet** magazine was first published in what year?

12. What do the books **The Dead Lecturer, The System of Dante's Hell** and **Blues People** have in common?

13. **What Manner of a Man,** written by Lerone Bennett, Jr., is a biography of whom?

14. Who was the first black American to publish a novel?

15. **On These I Stand** was a collection of whose works?

16. Name the author who won a Pulitzer Prize for his play **A Soldier's Story**.

17. What do **Pride's Castle, A Woman Called Fancy, The Foxes of Harrow** and **Floodtide** all have in common?

18. Whose autobiography is entitled **The Third Door**?

19. Whose autobiography is entitled **Along This Way**?

20. Who is the author of **Cotton Comes to Harlem**?

21. Whose autobiography is entitled **The Big Sea**?

22. What do **The Chinaberry Tree, There Is Confusion**, **Comedy, American Style** and **Plum Bun** have in common?

23. Who was the first black to be published in America?

24. Who wrote the film **Odds Against Tomorrow** (1959), which starred Harry Belafonte?

25. Who wrote the play **Star in the Morning** about the life of vaudeville entertainer Bert Williams?

26. What do **Stranger and Alone**, **To Make a Poet Black**, **The Lonesome Road**, and **No Day of Triumph** have in common?

27. Who was the first black war correspondent (Italio-Ethiopian War)?

28. Famed author James Baldwin hails from what city?

29. Whose final play was entitled **The Sign in Sidney Brustein's Window**?

30. Who was the first black to be admitted to the Senate and House press galleries?

31. The newspaper **Rights of All** was originally known by what name?

32. Who is called the "Father of Black American Art"?

33. Who was the winner of the 1952 National Book Award for **Invisible Man**?

34. Who assisted the late Malcom X with the writing of his life story?

35. Who wrote the novel **Knock On Any Door**?

36. Playwright Paulette Williams is better known by what name?

37. Who wrote the best selling novel **The Color Purple**?

38. Who wrote **Uncle Tom's Cabin**?

39. Who wrote the book **Trick Baby**?

40. What NBA player authored the book **Up for Glory**?

41. Who wrote the book **Daddy Cool**?

42. In 1964, Dick Gregory wrote the autobiography of his life. What was the name of it?

43. Who wrote the play **Amen Corner**?

44. Who was the writer of the philosophies and opinions of Marcus Garvey?

45. She has been called the leading black poet of our times. Who is she?

46. Name the TV producer who set up a program for young black writers to submit scripts for possible use on TV programs in the '70s.

47. Who is the author of **Manchild in the Promised Land**?

48. Who is the author of the book **Soul On Ice?**

49. **The Me Nobody Knows: Children's Voices from the Ghetto** was written in 1969 by what well-known author?

50. What was the title of Maya Angelou's autobiography?

51. The book **The 16th Round** was the life story of what boxer?

52. In 1965, this author wrote **The Way It Spozed to Be**. Name the author.

53. The film **The Cool World** was based on the book of the same title. Who wrote it?

54. He wrote about racial problems in the Boston school system in the '60s. Name him and his book.

55. **Black World** magazine had a different name when it first hit the stands. What was it?

56. In 1968, William Grier and Price Cobbs joined forces to produce what book?

7. Frederick Douglass worked his way from slave to free man in the mid-1800s. Among his many accomplishments, he established his own newspaper. What did he call it?

58. Who wrote the book **Black Like Me?**

59. Who wrote the book **Native Son?**

60. Who wrote the book **Growing Up Black**?

61. Who wrote **To Kill a Mockingbird**, the story of a black farmer falsely accused of raping a white woman?

62. Name the woman who wrote **Brown Girl, Brownstones**.

63. William Wells Brown was the first black author to have a play published. What was this work?

64. She wrote **On City Streets**. Who is she?

65. Who wrote the mid-'60s book entitled **Where Do We Go From Here**?

66. The title of this book also became Adam Clayton Powell's battle cry. What was it?

67. Name the two authors who compiled the **Adventures of the Negro Cowboy**.

68. What did tennis great Arthur Ashe title his autobiography?

69. Who wrote **The Autobiography of Miss Jane Pittman**?

70. Which former Supreme has written a book entitled **Dream Girl: My Life as a Supreme**?

71. Barry Beckham wrote what scholastic book?

72. Famed poet and Pulitzer Prize winner Gwendolyn Brooks is from what state?

73. What poem inspired Lorraine Hansberry's **Raisin in the Sun**?

74. Eric Monte had one of his books become a film and a TV series. Name the original book.

75. Who is the author of **Revolt of the Black Athlete**?

76. Lucille Giles took an interesting approach to her book for children about black history; she made it a coloring book. What was it called?

77. LeVar Burton played the title role in the TV movie **Dummy**. Who wrote the original book?

78. Name the former NBA great who wrote **Rockin' Steady: A Guide to Basketball and Cool**.

79. Fran Ross wrote a novel about a person who is called a four-letter word all blacks truly despise. Name the book.

80. Who wrote the book about slavery entitled **Before the Mayflower**?

81. Who wrote **The Appeal Against Slavery**?

82. What politically active woman of the '60s and '70s wrote **Women, Race and Class**?

83. Name the former Black Panther who wrote **Seize the Time**.

84. Who is the author of the children's book **Black Folktales**?

85. For years, Gary Coleman's medical ailments have made the news. A few years ago, Bill Davidson wrote a book about Gary's medical history. Name the book.

86. What is the name of the children's version of **Ebony** magazine?

87. Prior to **Gone With the Wind** in the 1930s, what was the most popular book sold in the US?

88. Novelist Kip Branch's first book was released late in 1981. What is it?

89. Ntozake Shange is the playwright who wrote one of the longest-titled, most dramatic plays of the '70s. Name this play.

90. Who wrote the **Journal of Negro History**?

91. W.E.B. DuBois, author of **The Souls of Black Folk**, is a famous historian. What does the "W.E.B." stand for?

PERSONALITIES

1. Whose real name was Lincoln Theodore Monroe Andrew Perry?

2. What is Butterfly McQueen's real first name?

3. Who was once known as "Sweet Mama Stringbean"?

4. James Arthur Johnson is the real name of what actor?

5. Who directed the film **Shaft**?

6. Who produced, directed and starred in **Sweet Sweetback's Badasssss Song** (1971)?

7. What is Fats Waller's real name?

8. After "The Twist," Chubby Checker popularized yet another dance. What was it?

9. What is Booker T's (of Booker T and the MG's) last name?

10. Who were the original Supremes?

11. What is Stevie Wonder's real name?

12. Name the three "Pips" from the group Gladys Knight and the Pips.

13. What is Little Richard's real name?

14. What is Satchel Paige's real first name?

15. Singer/Dancer/Actress Debbie Allen (**Fame**) debuted on Broadway in the chorus of what show?

16. Who won the Donaldson Award in 1946 as the most promising new performer of that year?

17. Most remember comedienne "Moms" Mabley, but what was her real first name?

18. Who was the star of the first all black talking movie, **Harlem Is Heaven**?

19. What was the first band with which Sarah Vaughan signed?

20. Famed vaudeville performer Bert Williams was once teamed with another performer from the days of vaudeville. Who was he?

21. Singer Ruth Jones was better known by what name?

22. Who was the first black star of the Metropolitan Opera?

23. A now famous actress/singer began her career as a soloist with the Katherine Dunham Dance Company. Who is she?

24. When he was four years old, he appeared in vaudeville with the Will Mastin Trio. Who is he?

25. What is Fats Domino's real name?

26. Name the person who replaced Diana Ross as lead singer of the Supremes.

27. Who was the first black to conduct the New York Philharmonic Orchestra?

28. Who was the first black performer to sing at La Scala?

29. Name all of Michael Jackson's sisters.

30. According to his ads for **Sports Illustrated**, what is Rosey Grier's hobby?

31. Alex Haley got his first big writing break with an interview for **Playboy** magazine. Whom did he interview?

32. His radio and TV boss Jack Benny always called him "Rochester." What was Rochester's full name?

33. What name was Malcolm X born with?

34. Who was called the "Play Doctor" on Broadway?

35. Two of the NBA's greatest centers were used in ads by TWA to advertise the leg room on that airline's planes. Name these two men.

36. What was Count Basie's first name?

37. He had a weekly network TV show and a weekly network radio show where he played the same role in the '80s. Name this actor.

38. What is Prince's full name?

39. The ventriloquial figure "Lester" is whose dummy?

40. Who was the first person to do a "Lite Beer from Miller" commercial?

41. Who is the smooth-voiced singer who for years has performed the Budweiser jingles?

42. Redd Foxx used to have a partner in his comedy routines. Name this man.

43. Jayne Kennedy once belonged to what group of dancers?

44. The ventriloquist Wayland Flowers has a black woman puppet who is just as sassy as Madame. What is her name?

45. Before he legally changed his name to Mr. T, what was his name?

46. Joe Louis was once an official goodwill ambassador for what Las Vegas hotel?

47. What comedian is known for being the "King of Rhymes"?

48. Muhammad Ali's Olympic gold medal, won in 1960, is not proudly displayed in his home. Where is it and why?

49. What is Smokey Robinson's real first name?

50. Who is called "The Queen of Soul"?

51. What does the "B.B." in B.B. King stand for?

52. Who originally were the "Savoy Big Five"?

53. Who was the first black to graduate from the University of Alabama?

54. Bob Dylan was once quoted as saying, "This man is America's greatest living poet." Who is he?

55. With whom did Billie Holiday cut her first record?

56. What was famed piano player "Jelly Roll" Morton's real first name?

57. Who was the founder of the Association for the Study of Negro Life and History (1915)?

58. Who was the executive secretary of the NAACP from 1931 to 1955?

59. Who was the organizer (1957) and a president (1968) of the Southern Christian Leadership Conference?

60. Who was the first black to earn a Ph.D from Yale University?

61. Poet LeRoi Jones is now better-known under another name. What is it?

62. Who is the current (1985) president of the United Negro College Fund?

63. Who organized the United Transport Service for Employees (1935)?

64. Who was the first black member of the Federal Reserve Board (1966)?

65. What is Flip Wilson's real first name?

66. Who was the first black to win the Nobel Peace Prize?

67. Name the black investigative reporter on "60 Minutes."

68. Who was the first black admiral (1971)?

69. Who was the first black professor at Harvard Medical School (1949)?

70. Who was the first black member of the Federal Communications Commission (1972)?

71. Who was the first American decorated by France (in WWI) with the Croix de Guerre?

72. Who founded the Black Muslims in 1931?

73. Name the black pilot who had to join the French Army during WWI to avoid US Army bigotry.

74. Who organized the Brotherhood of Sleeping Car Porters in 1925?

75. Who was the first black to sit on the National Security Council?

76. What is comedian Redd Foxx's real name?

77. Who is Delloreese Patricia Early?

78. Who is LaDonna Andrea Gaines?

79. LaToya Jackson has made guest appearances in two videos. One was "Say, Say, Say" with her brother and Paul McCartney. Name the other.

80. Who is the **Playboy** artist that, among his other monthly contributions, pens the "Horny Little Old Lady" cartoons?

81. Joe Black is one of America's most influential men; his syndicated commentary program, "By the Way," has spoken out for years on black life in America. Black is vice president of what large American company?

82. Joseph Gallo was called "Crazy Joe." Why?

83. Who was called "The Say Hey Kid"?

84. Quincy Jones' wife was the star of a '60s cop show. Name her and the show.

85. Name the TV personality who, as a small girl, had the popular line, "I love you, Mrs. Butterworth" in that syrup's commercial.

86. According to the old folk song, who was a "steel drum man"?

87. Name the R&B group that used to call itself "Chubby and the Turnpike."

88. What NBA star is called "The Human Highlight Film"?

89. Several years ago, Sugar Ray Leonard and his son, Sugar Ray, Jr. made a commercial for what popular soft drink?

90. For what shoe company did O.J. Simpson do ads?

91. Darrel Dawkins playfully claimed he was from what planet?

92. Who was the first athlete to be called "The Franchise"?

93. Who is the talented teenage dancer in the Pepsi commercial with the Jacksons?

94. Who is the internationally famous athlete nicknamed "The Black Pearl"?

95. What was the nickname of boxer Joe Louis?

POLITICS

1. Who was the first black to win an elec-
    tive office?

2. In what year did Congress authorize the
    enlistment of blacks for military service?

3. Who were Edward G. Walker and
    Charles L. Mitchell?

4. Who was the first black in the House of
    Representatives?

5. Who was the first black senator in the
    US?

6. Oscar De Priest was the first black con-
    gressman from what northern state?

7. Who was the first black woman state leg-
    islator?

8. Who was the first black to head a con-
    gressional committee?

9. Who was the first black to represent
    North Carolina in the state legislature?

10. What do Reese Hammond, Cecil A. Partee, Carl Stokes and Theodore Johnson all have in common?

11. Who do George W. Haley, Ivan Warner, Verda F. Welcome and Coleman A. Young all have in common?

12. In what year did black voters first cast their ballots in a presidential election?

13. Who was the first black woman to be elected to Congress?

14. Who was the first black cabinet member?

15. Who were Mercer Cook, Franklin Williams, Patricia Harris and James Nabrit?

16. Who was the first black Justice of the Supreme Court?

17. Who was the first black to sit in the US Senate in the 1900s?

18. Who headed the Montgomery Improvement Association in 1955?

19. Which Congressional District in New York did Adam Clayton Powell, Jr. first represent?

20. What president had the highest number of black appointments?

21. What do Richard Cain, Robert Elliott, Robert DeLarge and Robert Smalls have in common?

22. Who was the last black to serve in the House before Oscar De Priest?

23. Which Alabama congressman served as both editor and publisher of the **Montgomery Sentinel**?

24. Who was the first black congressman from Florida?

25. Who was the first black congressman from Georgia?

26. Who was the first black to represent Louisiana in the House of Representatives (1875)?

27. Who was the first black Democrat elected to Congress?

28. Which congressman was publisher and editor of **People's Voice**?

29. Who was the first black to serve on the House Judiciary Committee (1963)?

30. Which congressman's autobiography was entitled **From the Virginia Plantation To the National Capital**?

31. George Carrol, the first black mayor of Richmond, California, resigned in 1965 to become what?

32. Who was Dayton, Ohio's first black city commissioner?

33. Who was the national chairman of the Freedom Now Party (1963)?

34. Who was Eldrige Cleaver's running mate in 1968?

35. Dick Gregory ran for president on what ticket?

36. In what year was the Mississippi Freedom Democratic Party founded?

37. Who was the first black woman admitted to the bar in Pennsylvania?

38. In what capacity did Yvonne Burke serve in the 1972 Democratic National Convention?

39. Who was the US Deputy Assistant Secretary of State for Public Affairs from 1964 to 1970?

40. Who was the director of the Women's Bureau of the US Department of Labor from 1969 to 1974?

41. Who was the first black woman to serve in the New York State Senate?

42. When John Cashin ran for governor of Alabama in 1970, what was his profession?

43. In the early '70s, Richard Hatcher was the mayor of what city?

44. In 1904, who was the National Liberal Party's candidate?

45. In 1971, who was Richard Nixon's only black White House aide?

46. Who organized "People United to Save Humanity (PUSH)"?

47. When Barbara Jordan was elected to the House of Representatives in 1972, what state did she represent and what was her previous political position?

48. Who is the president/founder of the National Domestic Workers Union of America?

49. Mervyn Dymally and George Brown were the first blacks elected to what office?

50. Who was the first black to be elected to the Montana State Legislature?

51. Who was the first black to attend a White House Cabinet meeting?

52. What is the term given to South Africa's racist political system?

53. What is the name of Pennsylvania's first black woman judge?

54. Who was the first black to be racial advisor for the Department of the Interior (1934)?

55. What political position did Lisle Carter hold under President Lyndon Johnson (1966)?

56. In 1965, he helped found the Student Nonviolent Coordinating Committee. Who is he?

57. Who was the minister of information for the Black Panther Party?

58. Who was the US Ambassador to the United Nations between 1977 and 1979?

59. Who was elected mayor of Atlanta, Georgia in 1973?

60. Who was the first black federal judge?

61. Who was the ambassador to the United Nations between 1979 and 1981?

62. Who was the first black mayor elected in New Orleans?

63. Who was the first black to become a permanent member of a US delegation to the United Nations?

64. Who was the first black woman to be appointed to the United Nations?

65. Who was America's first black four-star general?

66. It was through whose advice that President Teddy Roosevelt began appointing blacks to government positions?

67. One of the most famous political incidents in the '70s involved the Wilmington Nine. In what state did the racial violence take place?

68. In 1967, President Johnson restruc-
    tured the Washington, DC city govern-
    ment. Name the man he appointed as
    that city's mayor.

69. President Ford, during the Bicentennial
    celebration, invited the president of
    Liberia for a visit. Name this man.

70. At the request of President Lincoln, this
    man urged New England area blacks to
    enlist in the Union Army. Name him.

71. What is the largest (in population) politi-
    cal nation in Africa?

72. Who is the current (1985) director of the
    NAACP?

73. Who is the only black appointed to a
    Cabinet post by Ronald Reagan?

74. Of what city was Carl Stokes once
    mayor?

75. The late Adam Clayton Powell, Jr. was
    the first black to act as chairman of the
    Education and Labor Committee. Re-
    cently, another black congressman was
    chosen to head that committee. Name
    him.

76. Who is the mayor of Philadelphia
    (1985)?

77. Name the actor/singer who kissed
    President Nixon (on the cheek) for a
    publicity photo.

78. Name the Assistant Secretary of Labor in the Nixon administration who was the highest ranking black appointed by the former president.

79. Who is the mayor of Washington, DC?

80. What state has had the largest number of black mayors?

81. The mayor of Newark, New Jersey is used to "running"; in fact, he is the only black mayor to complete the Boston Marathon, held every year in April. Name this political runner.

82. 1984 Nobel Prize winner Desmond Tutu invited an American senator to his native land of South Africa. Name this senator.

83. Third party presidential candidates rarely get media attention, but when Dick Gregory ran in 1968, his political pamphlet caused a stir. What was special about it?

84. Julian Bond was a member of the legislature of which state?

85. What is the Spingarn Medal?

86. In what year did Elijah Muhammad found the Black Muslims?

87. Name the president who signed into law the Civil Rights Act.

88. Who was the last president to own slaves?

89. In what movie would you find William Marshal playing then Massachusetts Attorney General Ed Brooke?

90. Who was nicknamed "The First American Negro Martyr"?

91. Name the British statesman who led that country's quest to end slavery.

92. What US president was "suspected" of being black because of his dark complexion?

FILM

1. Who played the part of Josephus in Mel Brooks' **History of the World — Part One**?

2. James Hall and Irene Delroy played a bickering couple in what film?

3. Name the John Ford film from 1960 that starred black actor Woody Strode.

4. Name the performer who, along with comic actor Stubby Kaye, sang "The Ballad of Cat Ballou."

5. What film won the 1967 Academy Award for Best Picture?

6. George Jackson was an inmate at San Quentin; his younger brother and a judge were killed at the Marin County Courthouse. Name the film based on this incident.

7. Name the film that was loosely based on the life of baseball hero Satchel Paige.

8. Who portrayed football great Gale Sayers in the TV film **Brian's Song**?

9. What do the films **The Man Who Fell to Earth**, **Revenge of the Nerds**, **Never Say Never Again** and **Sharkey's Machine** all have in common?

10. Who portrayed Idi Amin in the film **Raid on Entebbe**?

11. Howard E. Rollins, Jr. made his screen debut as a Coalhouse Walker in what film?

12. Winston Zeddmore was the only black . . . what?

13. What do the films **No Way Out**, **The Jackie Robinson Story**, **Edge of the City** and **Raisin in the Sun** have in common?

14. In what film did Sammy Davis, Jr. make his acting debut?

15. Who was the first black woman to sign a term contract in films?

16. Who was the first American to be presented with an honorary membership in the Norwegian Society of Artists?

17. What now famous black actor made his Off Broadway debut in the play **Wedding in Japan** (1957)?

18. Hattie McDaniel was the first black woman to win the Oscar—for what film?

19. Frederick O'Neal helped found what famous organization?

20. What now-famous actor was the first black All American football player?

21. What do the films **Cabin in the Sky**, **The Member of the Wedding**, **The Sound and the Fury**, and **Cairo** have in common?

22. "I'm Just Wild About Harry," written by the late Eubie Blake, came from what all-black musical?

23. In what film did Stepin Fetchit play the role of "Gummy"?

24. **Sanders of the River** starred what famous black actor?

25. Bill Robinson and Shirley Temple starred together in what two 1935 films?

26. Louise Beavers starred as Toinette, an ex-slave, in what film?

27. Freddi Washington starred as Louise Beavers' daughter in what 1934 film?

28. What was Eddie "Rochester" Anderson's last film?

29. Cab Calloway, Lena Horne and Fats Waller starred together in what movie musical?

30. Who replaced Stepin Fetchit in the **Charlie Chan** film series?

31. Which film stars Beatrice Pearson and Mel Ferrer and is about a family that passes for white?

32. Actress Dorothy Dandridge had a bit part in which classic Marx Brothers' film?

33. What is the name of the fighter who falls in love with Carmen in the film **Carmen Jones**?

34. In what play/film would you find the character of "Sportin' Life"?

35. James Earl Jones played a bombardier in his first movie role. Name the film.

36. In what 1968 film did Jim Brown star with actress Raquel Welch?

37. What do the films **Doctors' Wives**, **The Landlord**, **Ensign Pulver** and **Georgia, Georgia** have in common?

38. What 1969 film had blacks taking over an advertising agency?

39. What is "Shaft's" first name?

40. What was the follow-up to the film **Super Fly**?

41. Cicely Tyson received an Academy Award nomination for what 1972 film?

42. What do the films **Myra Breckenridge**, **Leo the Last**, **Cotton Comes to Harlem** and **Halls of Anger** have in common?

43. What 1967 film featured Beah Richards and Robert Hooks as mother and son?

44. Which all-black revue introduced the "Charleston"?

45. The Academy Award for Best Supporting Actor of 1982 went to what actor for his role in **An Officer and a Gentleman**?

46. He was called "The Black Valentino." Who was he?

47. The film **Imitation of Life**, the story of a light-skinned black woman who tries to pass as white, was remade about twenty years later. What was the title of the remake?

48. Who played Joe Louis in the film **Spirit of Youth**?

49. Who played the role of the black farmer falsely accused of rape in **To Kill a Mockingbird**?

50. Who sang the title song to the Steve McQueen film **Cincinnati Kid**?

51. Name the three films that starred Richard Widmark and Sidney Poitier.

52. Who played James Bond's pal Felix Lighter in **Never Say Never Again**?

53. Who played the vampire in **Blackula**?

54. What was Eddie Murphy's first major movie?

55. Gladys Knight has starred in one film during her career. Name it.

56. Who played the motorcycle daredevil in the disaster film **Earthquake**?

57. Who played the maid of Spencer Tracy and Katherine Hepburn in the film **Guess Who's Coming to Dinner**?

58. Name the two films for which Michael Jackson has sung the title theme.

59. Name the actress who played opposite Charlton Heston in the movie **The Omega Man**.

60. Name the film Eddie Murphy starred in before **Beverly Hills Cop**.

61. The group Shalimar contributed their musical talents to what popular 1984 film?

62. A Southern town is torn apart by racial strife until a combined effort by whites and blacks to rescue a little black girl makes them forget their hatred. Name this film.

63. He was "The Duke of New York" in the movie **Escape from New York**. Name him.

64. In what film will you find Reverend Jesse Jackson, the Staple Singers and Richard Pryor?

65. In which Frank Sinatra film would you find Sugar Ray Robinson playing a cop?

66. In what film does Dan Ackroyd introduce James Brown as "the hardest working man in show biz"?

67. Who played the train conductor in **Silver Streak**?

68. What was the name of the pimp in the movie **The Mack**?

69. What was the name of the club Prince played in the movie **Purple Rain**?

70. Who played Captain Terril in **Star Trek II**?

71. Who played the blind deejay "Super Soul" in the film **Vanishing Point**?

72. In which James Bond film does Bond have a black lover?

73. What is Billy Dee Williams' character's name in the **Star Wars** films?

74. Who is the NBA great that starred in the film **The Fish That Saved Pittsburgh**?

75. In the movie, **Cornbread, Earl and Me**, who was the NBA star that played Cornbread?

76. Who played the role of the security guard in **The Towering Inferno**?

77. In John Wayne's last film, **The Shootest**, who played the blacksmith?

78. Name the two stars of **The Skin Game**, a movie about a pair of con men playing slave and slave owner.

79. Name the film that featured the music of the great ragtime musician Scott Joplin.

80. Roberta Flack, the Jackson Five, Wilson Pickett, the late Marvin Gaye and many

others starred in this 1972 film shot at an exposition in Chicago. Name the movie.

81. Name the movie starring Burt Lancaster in which Ossie Davis played a super-smart slave.

82. Who played James Caan's trainer in the film **Rollerball**?

83. In the **Rocky** films, what were Appollo Creed's two nicknames?

84. Name the male and female leads of the movie **The River Niger**.

85. In the star-studded cast of **Victory at Entebbe**, who played Idi Amin?

86. Who played the government agent in the James Coburn film **The President's Analyst**?

87. Name the actor who played Spear-chucker in the movie **M*A*S*H**.

88. Who sang the title track to **The Love Machine**?

89. Jim Brown, Jim Kelly and Fred Williamson made one film together. Name it.

90. What Kool and the Gang song was in **Saturday Nite Fever**?

91. In what comedy hit will you hear the line, "I like my coffee black, like my men"?

92. Dorothy Dandridge did not do her own singing in the movie **Carmen Jones**. Who dubbed her voice?

93. Who played Sam in the film **Casablanca**?

94. Boxer Ken Norton played a strong-willed slave in two films of the mid-'70s. Name both.

95. In the film **Airplane, the Sequel**, the ticket scalper wears a baseball cap from what team?

96. NBA great Bernard King and "Hill Street Blues's" Mike Warren teamed up with Gabe Kaplan in what movie?

97. Name the actress who played the sexy tease in the movie **Frogs.**

98. "Magnum P.I.'s" pal Roger E. Mosley played a role in the film version of Muhammad Ali's life, **The Greatest**. Who did Mosley play?

99. Boxing great Archie Moore played a slave named Jim in what film?

TV/RADIO

1. Irene Cara's "fame" started when she was a youngster on what television show?

2. Name the hip, black muppet on "Sesame Street" who became famous by singing about the "Days of the Week."

3. Name the cartoon series based on "Amos 'n' Andy."

4. "The Banana Splits Adventure Hour" featured a weekly segment entitled "Danger Island." What was the name of the person (already living on the island) who befriended Link Simmons?

5. Name Michael's two pet mice and his snake from the cartoon series "The Jackson Five."

6. On what show would you find Rudy, Weird Harold, Mush Mouth and Russell?

7. Leonard Evans was the first black to produce a radio series. Name the show.

8. Who played "Birdie" on "The Great Gildersleeve" series?

9. Ethel Waters, who originally played "Beulah," was replaced by what famed actress?

10. Arthur Godfrey featured a black singing group on his radio show. Name the group.

11. Who was the only black performer in the cast of the NBC "Opera Television Theatre" presentation of "Tosca" (1955)?

12. In the television series "Julia," what was the name of Julia's son?

13. Who were the announcer and orchestra leader for "The New Bill Cosby Show" (CBS)?

14. "Sanford and Son" was based on what British TV show?

15. Who played the financial consultant/ lawyer on the first season of "Silver Spoons"?

16. Who sang the theme to the TV show "Baretta" ("Keep Your Eye On the Sparrow")?

17. Who did the theme music to the series "The Men"?

18. Demond Wilson, Denise Nicholas and Kim Fields starred in a comedy about a father who had deserted his family, only to return and find his wife had declared him legally dead. What was the series?

19. Who starred as Paul Bratter on ABC's short-lived version of "Barefoot in the Park"?

20. Which two actresses played Chet Kincaid's mother on the original "The Bill Cosby Show"?

21. What was the name of Bernie Steinberg's cab driver friend on "Bridget Loves Bernie"?

22. Actor Kene Holliday starred in what comedy set in the fictional town of Clinton Corners?

23. In what television series did actor Todd Bridges co-star before "Diff'rent Strokes"?

24. In what series did singer/actress Della Reese co-star as the owner of Ed's Garage?

25. Before "Get Christie Love," actress Teresa Graves co-starred in a popular comedy series with Judy Carne and Goldie Hawn. What was the series?

26. For a short time, Nipsey Russell appeared in a situation comedy as Officer Anderson. Name the series.

27. Jimmie Walker starred as J.J. Evans on "Good Times." What did the "J.J." stand for?

28. Harrison Page starred in a comedy series with comedian Don Rickles. Name the series.

29. Whitman Mayo starred in what spin-off from "Sanford and Son"?

30. What was the name of Raymond Burr's bodyguard/aide on "Ironside"?

31. What is the full name of Ted Lange's character on "The Love Boat"?

32. Who played Lt. Ginger Ballis in the television series "M*A*S*H"?

33. What was the last name of Gordy, the weatherman at WJM on "The Mary Tyler Moore Show"?

34. Before "Good Times," John Amos played Esther Rolle's husband in another series. What was the show?

35. Who hosted a summer variety show with Melba Moore in 1972?

36. Greg Morris played an electronics expert on "Mission: Impossible." What was his character's full name?

37. Who was the boy Mork befriended in the first season of "Mork and Mindy"?

38. Jemal David (Otis Young) and Earl Corey (Don Murray) teamed up as bounty hunters in what show?

39. What series teamed actor Rupert Crosse with actor/comedian Don Adams?

40. Who was the orchestra leader on "The Pearl Bailey Show" (1971)?

41. For a time, actor Percy Rodriguez played Dr. Harry Miles on a "continuing" series. What was the show, and who played his wife?

42. During the first time actor Mike Evans left "The Jeffersons," he co-starred in another television series. Name the show.

43. "The Protectors," starring Hari Rhodes as a district attorney, was one of the shows that comprised what series?

44. On "Rhoda," what was the name of Joe Gerard's partner, and who played him?

45. On what movie was the the series "What's Happening?" based?

46. "Temperature's Rising," seen between 1972 and 1974, had three different casts/formats, but only one person made it through all three cast changes. Who was he?

47. In 1973, actor James McEachin starred as "Tenafly," a private detective. What was Tenafly's first name?

48. Who is Gordon Sims better known as?

49. On "Welcome Back Kotter," what was Freddie Washington's nickname?

50. On the show "Sanford and Son," Redd Foxx was always faking a heart attack. When he did, he grabbed his chest and screamed the name of his dead wife. What was her name?

51. There was a Dave Nelson on the TV show "Ozzie and Harriet," but on what TV detective show would you find Greg Morris playing Dave Nelson?

52. "Kunta Kinte" was changed to what name?

53. On "The Mod Squad," what was Lincoln Hayes' favorite comment?

54. Terry Carter has had four TV shows. Name them.

55. NBA on CBS has become a Sunday afternoon institution. Who was the first man to do the color commentary?

56. We have all seen Tony Chisom over and over again on TV. In what TV commercial does he appear?

57. What is the apartment number of "The Jeffersons"?

58. Marla Gibbs, who plays the role of Florence the maid on "The Jeffersons," tried a spin-off that lasted only a few weeks. Name the series.

59. Who was the first black emcee of a network game show?

60. On the United Negro College Fund commercials, what line is usually stated at the end?

61. Who was the first actor to win three successive Best Supporting Actor Emmys?

62. What parting words does Don Cornelius usually say at the end of "Soul Train"?

63. What were the names of James and Florida Evans' children on "Good Times"?

64. Name the butlers of the Tate family on "Soap."

65. On what network anchor desk will you find Beverly Williams?

66. On the TV show "Magnum, P.I.," what is the name of T.C.'s helicopter service?

67. On the TV series "Batman," Julie Newmar was one of two women to play Catwoman. Who was the other?

68. Name the two actors who played Lionel Jefferson.

69. Who is the black veejay on MTV?

70. Who played Oscar and Felix in the black version of "The Odd Couple"?

71. What was Fred Sanford's favorite singing group?

72. Name the Clifton Davis TV series in which he played a barber.

73. On the TV show "Barney Miller," what was the name of the book that Detective Harris wrote?

74. On what prime time series was the first interracial kiss on television?

75. On the cartoon show, "The Harlem Globetrotters," who was the voice of Meadowlark Lemon?

76. Who was the first black newsman on TV?

77. On the television series "Gimme a Break," Nell and Addy are best friends. What are their last names?

78. On the program "Don Kirshner's Rock Concert," what song was used for the show's opening?

79. On the Black Entertainment Network, who is the host of "Video Soul"?

80. Who is the informant used frequently by "Starsky and Hutch"?

81. Name the short-lived TV series that starred Ben Vereen and Jeff Goldblum.

82. What was the name of the black woman singer in the cartoon series "Josie and the Pussycats"?

83. Bill Crain was the first black director of an hour-long dramatic series. Name the company for which he worked?

84. What was the name of the butler on the TV show "The Big Valley"?

85. What TV character is famous for saying "What you talkin' about"?

86. What was the name of the black fighter pilot on "Battlestar Gallactica"?

87. What was the name of the maid on "The Danny Thomas Show"?

88. For years, Tony Brown has hosted his own talk show on the PBS network. What is the current name of his show?

89. Who hosted the magazine-format show "Today's Black Woman"?

90. This rotund funnyman was a regular on both "Laugh-In" and "Good Times." Name him.

91. This soft drink commercial was one of the most popular during the decade of the '70s. Name the product and the star.

92. On what children's show would you have found Mr. Baxter?

93. What was the name of George Jefferson's mother?

94. The producer of "The Wild Wild West" was one of the few TV producers in Hollywood to routinely use Blacks on a network series as extras and walk-ons. Who was he?

95. Before "What's Happening," actor Haywood Nelson starred in another short-lived TV series. What was it?

96. On what current (1985) TV series will you find actor Phillip Michael Thomas?

97. Leslie Uggams got her TV career start on what program?

98. In the early '70s, this young gentleman was a spokesperson for a national ham-

burger chain and even did a guest spot on several TV sitcoms, including "The Odd Couple." What is his name?

99. George Pal created a Gumby-like character in the early '50s. Name this black clay figure.

100. What was Sergeant Kinchloe's first name on the series "Hogan's Heroes"?

VINYL

1. What is Louis Armstrong's famed nick-name?

2. The year was 1958 and singer Tommy Edwards had a hit on the charts. What was the name of that tune?

3. Who produced Lesley Gore's early hits?

4. Before the Righteous Brothers had hits with "Ebb Tide" and "Unchained Melody," someone else had popularized these tunes. Name the singer.

5. Johnny Mathis has remained on what record label throughout his career?

6. Who was the first female singer to earn five gold records?

7. Sarah Vaughan's first single sold over two million copies. Name the song.

8. Who introduced the song "Variety Girl" in the film of the same name?

9. Who wrote the tune "Carry Me Back To Ol' Virginny"?

10. What is Cab Calloway's theme song?

11. Who had a hit record with the tune "Move On Up a Little Higher"?

12. Which recording group had five consecutive #1 records in 1965?

13. What was Chuck Berry's first single?

14. Lew Chudd was the founder of what record company?

15. Who recorded the original hit version of "Sea of Love"?

16. Who originally recorded "The Twist" (before Chubby Checker)?

17. What was Little Richard's first American hit?

18. Who had an original hit with "Twistin' the Night Away"?

19. What is Dionne Warwick's real first name?

20. What are the first names of the Pointer Sisters?

21. Clyde McPhatter was originally the lead singer of what group?

22. On which record label did Otis Redding record?

23. Who was the only R&B artist to appear at the "Monterey Free Festival" (1967)?

24. What does the "MG" signify in the group "Booker T and the MG's"?

25. The Marvelettes recorded the first #1 song for Motown Records. Name this tune.

26. Who recorded the hit "You Beat Me To the Punch"?

27. What was the Supremes' first single without Diana Ross?

28. When the Jackson Five left Motown, with which label did they sign?

29. What was the first group signed to the Tamla record label?

30. With whom did Marvin Gaye record before teaming up with Tammi Terrell?

31. When the Four Tops left Motown, with which record label did they sign?

32. In 1969, the Isleys formed their own record label. What was it?

33. "TSOP," featuring the Three Degrees on background vocals, was used as the theme for what popular television show?

34. Who recorded the hit tune "La La Means I Love You"?

35. Who recorded the hit "Mixed Up, Shook Up Girl"?

36. Who recorded the hit "Mashed Potato Time"?

37. Who recorded the hit tune "Rockin' Roll Baby"?

38. Who recorded the hits "Yakety Yak" and "Charlie Brown"?

39. Who recorded such hits as "Stagger Lee," "Personality" and "I'm Gonna Get Married"?

40. David Baughan, Bobby Hendricks, Charlie Hughes, Rudy Lewis and Johnny Moore were at one time members of what group?

41. The original members were Doris Kenner, Beverly Lee, Shirley Alston and Addie Harris. Name the group.

42. Who was the first black to win **Cash Box** magazine's "Best Male Vocalist" award?

43. Levi Stubbs, Abdul Fakir, Lawrence Payton and Renaldo Benson are better known as what?

44. DeDe Henry, Dolores Brooks, Patsy Wright and Barbara Alston are better known as what?

45. Her recording of "Down-Hearted Blues" in 1923 sold over two million copies. Who is she?

46. In 1974, this group broke the standing one-week attendance record Elvis Presley set for the city of Las Vegas. Name the group.

47. The Beatles re-did the song "Twist and Shout." Who sang the original?

48. This white group was hired to play the famed Apollo Theatre in Harlem because the booking agent thought they were black after hearing their records. Name the group.

49. What is James Brown's nickname drawn from a Marlon Brando film character?

50. Name the three artists who had hits with the Clifton Davis classic "Never Can Say Goodbye."

51. Who sang "Band of Gold"?

52. One of Bill Cosby's most famous routines deals with the removal of his tonsils. In that routine, what does he call an intern?

53. Michael Jackson won eight Grammys in 1984, breaking the record of six Grammys in one year. Whose record did he break?

54. Which Stevie Wonder song mentions the countries of Iraq and Iran?

55. Otis Williams and Melvin Franklin are the only two remaining original members of what world-renowned group?

56. The popularity of the songs "New York, New York" and "LA Is My Lady" inspired a song called "Hello, Detroit." Who wrote it?

57. What two Motown groups formed a group known as "The Magnificent Seven"?

58. What was the name of the hit song recorded by Gene Chandler in 1972?

59. "Hang on Sloopy" and "The In Crowd" were both instrumental hits by what artist?

60. Claudette Rogers, Bobby Rogers, Ronnie White and Pete Moore were once part of which group?

61. Cindy Birdsong, who replaced Florence Ballard as a member of the Supremes, had come from what popular group?

62. Ted White was the manager and husband of which popular singer?

63. The group's first album was "Are You Experienced," followed by "Axis: Bold As Love." Who were they?

64. What was Sly and the Family Stone's first single?

65. What was the first posthumous #1 hit in recorded music history?

66. What was the original name of the Fifth Dimension?

67. The Spinners' hit version of "Cupid" (1980) was coupled with what song?

68. Which record company did Gladys Knight and the Pips sign with after leaving Motown?

69. Who sang a duet with Donna Summer on "Heaven Knows"?

70. What is the name of B.B. King's guitar?

71. What was the only song from the movie soundtrack of **Sgt. Pepper's Lonely Hearts Club Band** to go gold?

72. What was the name of Natalie Cole's first hit?

73. Who recorded the 1972 hit "Walkin' In the Rain With the One I Love"?

74. Hazel Payne, Perry Kibble, Don Johnson and Janice Johnson all formed what popular group?

75. Who produced the Emotions' hit "Best Of My Love"?

76. He released an album entitled "Don't Mess With Mr. T" about ten years before the Mr. T of "The A-Team" became popular. Name this musician.

77. By what collective name do we know Ronnie, Kelley and Rudolph?

78. The song "Mr. Bojangles" (Bill Robinson's nickname) was sung by what white group?

79. These five young men began singing at a very early age and never let their sightlessness hinder their gospel career. Who are they?

80. In Joe Tex's song "Skinny Legs and All," what band member finally wound up with the lady who had the skinny legs?

81. Who is the only person to sing title themes to three different James Bond movies?

82. In both the Sam & Dave and the Blues Brothers version of "Soul Man," a band member's name is yelled out in the middle of the song, and he is told to "play it." In both versions, it's the same name. Who is it?

83. Her first album was titled "Inseperable." Name her.

84. Pigmeat Markham and Shortly Long each had a hit with a "judicial" song. Name the tune.

85. In the film **48 Hours**, what was the name of the black rock band?

86. The Famous Flames were the backup group for what well-known singer?

87. The song "Troglodyte" by The Jimmy Castor Bunch featured a cave woman named Bertha Butt. Who were her two sisters?

88. Who sang the early '50s song "Santa Baby"?

89. What was the first white group to sign with Motown Records?

90. What comedian who has, among his many credits, an album entitled "Don't Smoke Dope, Fry Your Hair"?

91. Who sang the early '70s hit, "Ooh, Child"?

92. Not to be confused with the blonde, pint-sized songwriter, the late Paul Williams was an original member of what famous group?

93. Who sang the song "Harry Hippie"?

94. The second most popular comedy team on black records were two overweight, raunchy, but very funny comedians. Name them.

95. Of all of the songs that Brook Benton has ever recorded, which sold the most copies?

96. Name the current rock group whose youthful sound reminds people of the early days of the Jackson Five.

97. Who sang the theme to the TV series "Maude"?

98. What was the first song that "rocketed" Billy Preston to the top of the charts?

99. What segment of "Soul Train" awards prizes to two teenage contestants if they can discover the names of famous musical artists concealed in a jumble of letters?

100. Charlie Pride sang the theme song to a film that starred Paul Newman and Henry Fonda in the early '70s. The song was "Kiss an Angel Good Morning." Name either title under which the movie was released.

SPORTS

1. In 1945, with which team did Jackie Robinson sign?

2. Joe Williams, a member of the Lincoln Giants, had two nicknames. What were they?

3. The "International League of Colored Baseball Clubs" changed their name to what?

4. On what date did the Negro Eastern League disband?

5. Who was known to steal regularly over a hundred bases each season?

6. The St. Louis Stars, the Detroit Stars, the Birmingham Black Barons and the Chicago American Giants were at one time part of what?

7. Who was the first black umpire in the major leagues?

8. Who was the first black coach of a major league sports team?

9. Who succeeded Ty Cobb as holder of the stolen base record?

10. Who was the first black heavyweight contender?

11. Under what name was boxer Melody Jackson known later in his career?

12. In 1951, he was the Eastern Golden Gloves 160-pound champ, but in 1952 he was the Eastern Golden Gloves 175-pound champ. Who was he?

13. In 1960, who was the National AAU Light Heavyweight champ, the National Golden Gloves Heavyweight champ and the Olympic Games Light Heavyweight champ?

14. Wilma Rudolph won three gold medals in the 1960 Olympics for which events?

15. Who was the first black golfer to win admission to the Professional Golfers Association?

16. Which black jockey rode his horse to victory in the first Kentucky Derby?

17. Who was the first black to play in the US Lawn Tennis Singles Championships?

18. Who was the last player in the NBA to win Rookie of the Year and MVP in the same season?

19. Name the player who has hit more lead-off homeruns than anyone else in baseball history.

20. What all-star shortstop was known as "Mr. Cub"?

21. What number did former Celtic great Bill Russell wear?

22. How many total homeruns did Henry Aaron hit in his career?

23. What active NFL running back has the nickname "Sweetness"?

24. Former Miami Dolphins' star Mercury Morris does not use the "Mercury" part of his name anymore, but his real first name. What is it?

25. Since 1950, who has won more American League batting titles than anyone else?

26. Who was the first non-quarterback to play at least twenty seasons in the NFL?

27. The 1979 World Champion Pirates adopted a popular song as their theme for the season. Name the song.

28. Only two players made over one million dollars playing for the 1984 New York Yankees. One was Dave Winfield. Who was the other?

29. During the '60s, who had the nickname "The World's Fastest Human"?

30. Name the only man to win the Heisman Trophy twice.

31. Over the past twenty years, what two of America's most popular sports have had double-headers?

32. What active baseball player has the most career homeruns of all active players?

33. During the decade of the '70s, only once did an American League player lead the majors in homeruns. Who was he?

34. Who was the first black golfer to play in the Masters?

35. Only one man in the history of the NBA has played for over ten seasons without ever fouling out of a game. Who is he?

36. Name the only man to play for the Globetrotters and the Boston Red Sox.

37. Who are the only two white men in the black athlete's Hall of Fame?

38. Rick Barry, former NBA and ABA star, always wore #24 whenever possible. Why?

39. A 1968 film inspired Walt Frazier's friends and fans to give him a classy nickname, due to the resemblance of Walt's wardrobe to the wardrobe of the film's star. What was this film?

40. Name the two black athletes who have been commentators on "Monday Night Football."

41. Who set the NFL single season reception record during the 1984 NFL season?

42. What was the last year a World Series team started an all-white line-up at all nine positions?

43. Who was the first black to compete for the World Billiards Championship?

44. Who was the first NBA rookie to be named MVP in an All-Star game (1959)?

45. The Buffalo Bills had a black quarterback in the mid-1960s. Who was he?

46. Name the two NBA teams for whom Artis Gilmore has played.

47. Wrestling great Ernie "The Cat" Ladd played for what former Super Bowl champions?

48. Who is the only man to play in the NBA, the ABA and for the Harlem Globetrotters?

49. Mickey Mantle is the leading switch-hitter of homeruns in baseball's history. Who holds second place?

50. Who is the all-time leading receiver in the NFL?

51. Who has been on the cover of **Sports Illustrated** more times than anyone else?

52. When Arthur Ashe won Wimbledon in 1975, whom did he beat in the finals?

53. What is the nickname of the Grambling sports teams?

54. What NFL back holds the record for scoring six touchdowns in one day?

55. Who was the first black player in the NBA?

56. Who was the first black player in the NHL?

57. Meadowlark Lemon left the Globetrotters to start his own basketball team. Name it.

58. Who won the CBS Slam-Dunk Competition?

59. Name the only man to lead both the American League and the National League in stolen bases.

60. Who is the only black baseball star to be named MVP on three separate occasions?

61. Which basketball star played with the Harlem Globetrotters before joining the Philadelphia Warriors in 1959?

62. Who was the first black tennis pro to play at Forest Hills?

63. Sweetwater Clifton, Reece Tatum and Marcus Haynes were members of what team?

64. Who was the first black heavyweight champion?

65. Who was the first black athlete to win an Olympic decathlon?

66. Up to and including Super Bowl #19, if the NFL maintains its current team

alignments, what is the only Super Bowl match-up that can never happen again?

67. Who was known as "The Ebony Antelope"?

68. In 1965, he had the highest number of free throws and was third in the league in scoring. Who is he?

69. Boxer Walker Smith was better known by what name?

70. What is Kareem Abdul Jabbar's original "full" name?

71. Who was Abraham Molineaux Hewlett?

72. Who established a new world record for the high jump in the 1956 Olympic Games?

73. What do Joshua Gibson, Satchel Paige, William Johnson, Monte Irvin and Buck Leonard all have in common?

74. Who was the first black American League winner of the MVP award?

75. Who was the first black player to be elected to the Baseball Hall of Fame?

76. Who was the first National League player to win the MVP award in two consecutive years?

77. Who is the first player to have won the MVP award in baseball in both leagues?

78. The first black college football game was played between which two schools?

79. Who was the first black captain of Notre Dame's football team?

80. Who received the Heisman Trophy in 1972?

81. Which football conference holds the distinction of being the last to integrate its teams?

82. Who was the first black to play pro football?

83. He wore #22 for the Baltimore Colts, and when he retired, his number was also retired. Who was he?

84. Who was the first black to win the Heisman Trophy?

85. Who was AFL Player of the Year in 1966? (Hint: he played for the Boston Patriots.)

86. Who was the first black captain of the Giants' football team?

87. Who was the sole black coach in the ABA during the 1972-1973 season?

88. Blacks comprised the entire first college All-American basketball team. In which season did this take place?

89. Who was the first black to play basketball on the University of Kentucky team?

90. Who was the first black to play for the University of Houston?

91. What is Sonny Liston's real first name?

92. Who was the first man in the US to win the Decathlon and Pentathlon in the same year (1941)?

93. Who was the first black high jumper to win an Olympic medal?

94. What has Harold Donovant done for the world of golf?

95. Who was the first black jockey to win first place at Saratoga Springs (1974)?

96. What boxer was nicknamed "The Barbados Demon"?

97. Which Boston-born boxing great won championships in the '40s and '50s, but did not get elected to boxing's Hall of Fame until the '70s?

98. What school did Julius Erving attend?

99. In professional baseball, what man has hit over 960 homeruns?

CURRENT EVENTS

1. What is the name of the Broadway play loosely based on the career of the Supremes?

2. What is the name of NASA's first black astronaut?

3. What was the nickname Reverend Jesse Jackson gave to his 1984 Presidential campaign?

4. What was the name of the only American band to join Band-Aid, the group formed from several of rock music's biggest acts that produced an album whose proceeds were given to the famine victims of Ethiopia?

5. Who was the pilot held captive by Syria that Jesse Jackson helped to release through his influence?

6. Who is the first black to be appointed to the Mississippi Supreme Court?

7. Who won the match race between Franco Harris and Jim Brown?

8. Name the outspoken black gentleman whose comments about black unity during Reverend Jesse Jackson's election bid received national attention.

9. Name the man who allegedly shot four attackers in New York during Christmas of 1984.

10. The Fiesta Bowl is a yearly occurrence; in 1984, the Bowl elected its first black Bowl Queen. Name her.

11. Several health and beauty aid companies recently began a campaign entitled "The Proud Lady." To whom are they referring?

12. Where was the first stop on the Jacksons' Victory Tour?

13. Name the coach of the Georgetown Hoyas who lead his team to the NCAA Championship in 1984.

14. ABC decided to replace O.J. Simpson for its telecast of the 1985 Super Bowl. Who was O.J.'s substitute?

15. In 1984, a black man was among the top ten Heroes of the Year. Who was he?

16. What city was host to the 1985 Black Film Festival?

17. Name the woman who finished out Vanessa Williams' term as Miss America.

18. Name the former NFL player who has been on the anchor desk of CBS's NFL

Sunday broadcasts for the last ten seasons.

19. A TV movie entitled "The Atlanta Child Murders" dealt with the man accused of the killings. What is his name?

20. Why did the BBC censor Tina Turner's hit song "Private Dancer"?

21. What was Weird Al Yankovich's take-off on Michael Jackson's hit "Beat It"?

22. Who shared the cover of **Penthouse** magazine with Vanessa Williams on the two occasions she appeared there?

23. Kareem Abdul Jabbar is the #1 all-time scoring leader in the NBA. What active player just became #3 on the list?

24. In what recent film would you hear the Kid Creole song "Male Curiosity"?

25. The leader of Lybia has been encouraging American blacks to take up arms and revolt against white America. What is his name?

26. In one of his recent movies, Richard Pryor mentions he will never use the word "nigger" again. What inspired this move?

27. The McDonald's Corporation has recently aired radio commercials aimed at the black market in which the company has given themselves a nickname. What is the nickname?

28. Stevie Wonder, Bob Dylan, Ray Charles, Lionel Ritchie and over three dozen other artists recently recorded a song, the proceeds from which will go to the starving peoples of Africa and the United States. Name this song.

29. Name the author of the recent book **The Man Behind the Laughter**.

30. At what fast-food chain do the Fat Boys "pig out" in the video version of their hit song "In Jail"?

31. **Good Housekeeping** magazine recently published the results of a poll to determine America's most eligible bachelors. Who was the only black man in the top ten on the list?

32. During Black History Month in 1985, this former Miss America narrated several TV spots about famous black Americans. What is her name?

33. Name the company that makes "Mr. T Cereal."

34. The country of Ethiopia has been getting world-wide assistance during its recent famine. What is that country's capital?

35. Who played Prince's father in the movie **Purple Rain**?

36. The Specials, a British multi-racial rock group, sang a song that became the theme for the riots that rocked Liverpool in the 1980s. Name the song.

37. Who won the award in 1984 for Black Athlete of the Year?

38. Over the last few years, which black pro has captained America's Davis Cup team?

39. Of the five main branches of the Armed Services, which has the fewest black recruits?

40. In 1984, the Pepsi-Cola Company used the Jacksons in its commercials; in 1985 to what popular singer did Pepsi turn?

41. Who is O.J. Simpson's usual partner in the Hertz Rent-a-Car ads?

42. Who were the hosts of the 1984 Black Achievement Awards?

43. Who played Jesse Owens in the 1984 TV movie about the life of the track star?

44. Name the current R&B group that is said to recapture the sound of the early Jackson Five.

45. Name the athlete who made the most money in 1984.

46. Who was the man who organized politicians and celebrities to demonstrate at the South African embassy in Washington in 1985?

47. Two famous singers who recently passed away were the subject of a Commodores single, "Nightshift.' Name the singers.

48. **Playgirl** magazine listed the top ten sexiest men of 1985 (in its perspective). Name the only two black men on the list.

49. What R&B group won top honors at the 1985 (14th Annual) Tokyo Music Festival?

50. What American city was the backdrop for the ten-hour Live Aid broadcast?

51. Name the actress/comedienne whose one-hour, one-woman special on HBO has won rave reviews in the summer of 1985.

52. What happened on Good Friday (April 5th), 1985 at 10:50 EST?

53. Who won the 1985 NBA MVP award in the finals?

54. What pitcher yielded Rod Carew's 3000th hit?

MISCELLANEOUS

1. What is the term—rarely used anymore —that refers to someone of mixed Caucasian and Negro blood?

2. Who was the first woman dance star with the Metropolitan Opera?

3. Who was the first black woman White House correspondent?

4. Who was the first black president of the National Education Association?

5. Name the first black graduate nurse in the US.

6. Name the first president of the National Association of Colored Women.

7. Who was the first woman bank president?

8. Who sang the theme to the film **The Bingo Long Traveling All-Stars and Motor Kings**?

9. Who was the first black to appear with any regularity on Broadway?

10. Who coined the term "Afro-American"?

11. Who was the first black Navy ensign (1942)?

12. Who was the first black deputy police commissioner of New York City (1951)?

13. Over fifty years ago, Dr. Alvin Loving became what major US city's first black high school teacher?

14. What was the name of the sometimes colorful, loose-fitting shirts worn in the late '60s and early '70s?

15. During the Christmas season, some blacks prefer to celebrate what African holiday?

16. Among the many newspapers this gentleman published was **The Negro World**. Who is he?

17. Name the actor who is married to Aretha Franklin.

18. Name the computer wizard in the comic strip "Bloom County."

19. What is the pen name used by author Robert Beck?

20. For what company did Lola Falana pose as a tigress in commercials?

21. On what label does Redd Foxx usually record?

22. When he was a spokesperson for Panasonic, what did Reggie Jackson rename "Omnivision"?

23. What is the name of Charlie Brown's black friend?

24. Famed Boston area artist John Wilson was commissioned by the city of Buffalo to sculpt the statue of what famous black American?

25. When blacks got the vote in the mid-1860s, why did they usually vote Republican?

26. When Louis Armstrong played the trumpet, he always had another object in his hand. What was it?

27. Who is Prince E. Hunt?

28. Edwin Moses and Mary Lou Retton shared the honor of being **Sports Illustrated** "Sports Persons of the Year" for 1984. The last time two people shared this honor was several years ago. Name the two individuals involved.

29. Who was billed as the "World's Largest Gospel Singer"?

30. The TV show "The White Shadow" took place at Carver High. What Los Angeles area high school was used for the exterior filming?

31. What state has the highest percentage of blacks, according to the 1980 census?

32. Washington, DC is where you will find the African Art Museum, the only museum in the US devoted solely to the study and exhibition of African art. In the 1880s, to whom did the building that houses this museum belong?

33. Name the black fighter who lost in the finals to Art Long in the film **Tough Enough**.

34. A "militant" elderly group borrowed their name from a militant black organization. Modified slightly, what is the name of the elderly group?

35. Who is called "Mr. October"?

36. What were the two reasons the Black Panthers were created?

37. For what was Moms Mabley always looking?

38. Name the woman who became a millionaire in the late 1800s with a conditioner to straighten kinky hair.

39. Complete this old phrase: "If you're white, you're right. . . ."

40. What was the two-word term given to the laws used to oppress black voters in the 1800s and early 1900s?

41. Name the baseball pitcher fined by his team because he wanted to wear curlers under his cap (for his California curls).

42. In wrestling, who was Tony Atlas' tag team partner?

43. Where was the favorite meeting spot (not for drinking) of most black men in their communities?

44. When the comedy team of Martin and Rossi broke up, with whom did Steve Rossi team up?

45. Who played Aunt Esther on "Sanford and Son"?

46. Name the black comic book character who shoots lightning bolts.

47. Name the black officer in Beetle Bailey.

48. Elmo Wright, formerly of the Kansas City Chiefs, was the first player to do what?

49. What American city has the highest percentage of blacks?

50. Who is the black female singer who had a cameo appearance in Ray Parker, Jr.'s "Ghostbusters" video?

51. The Americas, Europe, Asia, Australia and Africa are represented in what world-renowned symbol?

52. What US currency is alleged to have a black person on it?

53. For years, South Africa has been selling a gold coin to US collectors. Dozens of groups have protested its sale in the US because of that country's political policies. Name the coin.

54. What was the name of the 1982 film which documented the growth of gospel music in the US?

55. On the western coast of Africa, there is a country called Liberia. The capital of that country is named after an American president. Which one?

56. During the 1970s, one of the richest women in rock music sang the song, "Angela," a tribute to black activist Angela Davis. Name this singer.

57. What European country is the closest to Africa?

58. Which African country has on its flag in the center a picture of a hand holding a torch?

59. In which war did the greatest number of black soldiers die fighting for the United States?

60. What is the name of the TV show hosted by Nipsey Russell on the Black Entertainment Network?

61. Who produced Sheena Easton's album entitled "Private Heaven"?

62. Since 1960, what man has the most World Series wins?

63. Name the popular magazine started by Earl Graves.

64. What is the term used by most businesses to show they consider blacks and

other minorities equally with white applicants?

65. In an interview, the Temptations gave credit to another group for the famed quintet's smooth dance steps. What group did they name?

66. Name the now-defunct TV show on which Vanessa Williams made her acting debut.

67. Lionel Ritchie's "All Night Long" video was produced by a former member of the 1960s band, the Monkees. What is his name?

68. Which became law first: the Voting Rights Act or the Civil Rights Bill?

69. In the Motown Classics commercial, how many albums are offered?

70. To promote his match with wrestler Antonio Onoki, Muhammed Ali attended a match in which—through a series of events—Ali was thrown out of the ring by another wrestler. What is his name?

71. In what country will you find the Owen Falls Dam?

72. In 1983, this black Frenchman won his country's top tennis tournament, the French Open. He is one of the best players in the world. Who is he?

73. Name the three New England states that made Martin Luther King's birthday a holiday before the government.

74. When is National Freedom Day, the day in 1865 when slavery was abolished?

75. Name the two seas which are located across the northern part of Africa.

76. Famed network newscaster Max Robinson is employed by which network?

77. In what TV series did Louis Gossett, Jr. star?

78. What two countries have the highest number of black men and women in prison?

79. Whenever Rick James performs, he gives the "hook 'em horns" finger sign. What else does that gesture mean?

80. Three NBA players share the nicknames of the Seven Dwarfs. Name them and the teams they play for.

81. Bert Jones in a "Lite Beer from Miller" commercial unsuccessfully tries to emulate one of his colleagues by smashing a beer can. Who is he trying to copy?

82. During the credits of two films released in the past three years, you can hear classic Nat King Cole songs. Name the films and their songs.

83. Name the two finalists in the CBS "One On One" sports competition.

84. What is the term used by businesses to show they give promotions with strong consideration to minority applicants?

85. In the film **Blazing Saddles**, when the white railroad foreman suggests that the black workers sing a "work song," what song does Cleavon Little and the other workers begin to sing?

86. What was the first name-brand doll to be offered in either a white or black version?

87. Jim Brown has been quoted as saying he has the most respect for what current NFL running back?

88. Name the former baseball player who once said that the white stones in the necklace he wore were second basemen's teeth.

89. Who portrayed the slain Egyptian leader Anwar Sadat in the TV movie based on his life?

90. If you were reading **Le Nouveau Monde** newspaper, in what country would you be?

91. What two countries were located at the site of present-day Tanzania?

92. According to census reports, which New England state has the smallest black population?

93. Before he chose the name Muhammad Ali, Cassius Clay considered another name. What was it?

94. Although he has long since been exiled, what country did Idi Amin lead?

95. What was the #1 newspaper for American Muslims in the late 1960s and 1970s?

96. The Gumbel brothers are each doing well in their respective network jobs. What are their first names?

97. From what country did the Bahamas gain their independence during the early 1970s?

98. Who wrote the state song of Virginia, "Carry Me Back to Ol' Virginny"?

99. What was the nickname of the late Haitian president, Francois Duvalier?

100. Name the beauty magazine aimed at today's black woman.

101. Name the two NBA stars who appear in an anti-smoking commercial.

102. Name the three largest countries of Africa whose names begin with the letter "Z."

103. Marvin Hagler has appeared in commercials warning Americans not to do something—what?

104. Called "a minority" in South Africa, the black population actually far and away outnumbers that nation's white population. How many blacks live in South Africa?

105. **Jet** Magazine now calls their listing of the top records on the charts the "**Jet**'s

Top 20 Singles." What was it called before?

106. What is the capitol of Uganda?

107. What is the official language of Zambia?

PICTURES

1. Who is this man?

2. Of what city is he the mayor (1985)?

3. This Tony Award-winning actor has been in a variety of films over the last several years, including **The Muppets Take Manhattan**, **The Cotton Club**, and the movie from which the photo was taken. It starred Chevy Chase. Name the film and the actor.

4. Who is this man?

5. Of what state was he the senator?

6. Richard Roundtree and Irene Cara co-starred with Burt Reynolds and Clint Eastwood in a detective spoof released at Christmas time in 1984. Name the film.

7. What song began Irene Cara's career?

8. In how many movies did Richard Roundtree play Shaft?

9. Who is this man?

10. Of what city is he the mayor (1985)?

11. Of what world-wide event in 1984 was he the host?

12. Name the film Sammy Davis Jr. and his friends made together.

13. With which well-known performer has Sammy been touring lately?

14. Name this popular actor.

15. In which Super Bowl did he play?

16. This well-known actor played Barney Collier for seven seasons on the TV series "Mission Impossible." Then he went on to play Lieutenant Dave Nelson on the TV series "VEGA$." Name him.

17. His colleagues on the show, Bart Braverman and Phylis Davis, and the star of the show, Robert Urich, all worked for what Las Vegas hotel?

18. Name this former US Ambassador to the United Nations.

19. Of what US city is he the current mayor (1985)?

20. Name this actress.

21. Recently the USA Network started showing her old TV series. Name the show.

22. K.C. Jones has been head coach of the Boston Celtics for several years, but he is better known in most circles for the national TV ads he does for what product?

23. Hank Aaron was once quoted as saying this man would be the one to break his record of 755. Who is he?

24. Name this popular singing group of the '50s.

25. Who is this mellow-toned singer?

26. Name this black leader of the early to mid-'60s.

27. Little Richard has chosen another profession over music. What is it?

28. Jimi Hendrix was considered the greatest rock guitarist of his day. He was also one of the first to do something to his guitar after a concert. What was it?

29. This is General Roscoe Robinson Jr. From what academy did he graduate?

30. This man was a pioneer for black performers entering the world of country-western music. Name him.

ANSWERS

HISTORY

1. William Tucker (1624)

2. Elias Neau

3. James Varick

4. **Freedom's Journal** (first published March 16, 1927)

5. A black man who crossed the Delaware with George Washington

6. The Free African Society

7. Philadelphia, 1787

8. Philadelphia, 1816

9. Philadelphia, 1794

10. **Mirror of Liberty** (published in New York City, 1838)

11. Macon B. Allen (Worcester, Massachusetts, 1845)

12. Harriet Tubman

13. James Augustine Healy

14. John Rock (1865)

15. Charlotte E. Ray

16. John Roy Lynch (Republican Convention, 1884)

17. Provident Hospital (Chicago)

18. Boston, 1900

19. New York City, 1909

20. Mary McLeod Bethune

21. Jane Bolin (1939)

22. 1964

23. Alcorn College

24. Benjamin O. Davis, Sr.

25. The Southern Christian Leadership Conference

26. 1944 (New York City)

27. The Thirteenth, 1865

28. Washington, DC, 1897

29. Gertrude Elise Ayer (1935)

30. Granville T. Woods

31. The African Methodist Episcopal Church

32. Booker T. Washington (1940)

33. They have all been black newspapers in the US.

34. Pinkerton

35. Marian Wright Edelman (1966)

36. One of the founders of the Mississippi Freedom Democratic Party

37. Jewel Stradford Lafontant (1955)

38. Edith S. Sampson (1950)

39. Virginia, 1619

40. The Universal Negro Improvement Association (1920)

41. Fifteenth

42. W.E.B. DuBois

43. The National Association for the Advancement of Colored People (NAACP)

44. 99th Pursuit Squadron

45. The day (May 17, 1954) when the Brown family won a suit against the Topeka Board of Education that allowed their daughter to attend an all-white school

46. He was the navigator of the **Nina** (one of Columbus' ships)

47. The founder of Chicago

48. John Derham

49. Heroic soldiers who fought at the Battle of Bunker Hill

50. 1752

51. The first black to graduate from an American college (Bowdoin)

52. July 28, 1868

53. Mississippi (Revels, 1870-1871; Bruce, 1875-1881)

54. Booker T. Washington

55. Robert Abbott

56. The first two Americans who were decorated for bravery in WWI (both were black)

57. A black man who was the first to die in the Boston Massacre

58. Dr. Martin Luther King, Jr.

59. Roland Hayes (1917)

60. William Grant Still (conducting the L.A. Philharmonic at the Hollywood Bowl, 1936)

61. On the 100th anniversary of the birth of Abraham Lincoln

62. 1910 (in New York City)

63. Berlin, Germany in 1936

64. Dr. Ralph Bunche

65. 1793

66. Oxford, Pennsylvania (Lincoln University)

67. Alabama

68. The Pilgrims, arriving on the Mayflower

69. Isabella

70. **Brown** v. **The Board of Education**

71. Slavery

72. 1883

73. **The Liberator**

74. Nat Turner

75. Moses (for leading people to "The Promised Land" of the North)

76. Napoleon

77. 1950

78. Monroe, Virginia

79. John Carlos and Tommie Smith

80. Charles Drew

81. The traffic light

82. Because both Frederick Douglass' and Abe Lincoln's birthdays fall in that week

83. Marcus Garvey (1919)

84. Alexander Graham Bell

85. Holland

86. Washington, DC

87. The United States Military Academy at West Point

88. Tobacco

89. Sympathy for the parents of the slain children who were victims of Atlanta mass murderer Wayne Williams.

90. Roy Wilkins

91. He was a white officer in charge of all-black troops.

92. The Coast Guard

93. "Black is Beautiful"

94. Nat King Cole

95. Muhammad Ali

96. Bessie Smith

LITERATURE

1. Lorraine Hansberry

2. **The Homesteader**

3. His poetry

4. A former slave who became one of New England's best known poets

5. **A Raisin in the Sun** (1959)

6. Gwendolyn Brooks

7. Arna Bontemps

8. Richard Wright

9. Dorothy West

10. James Baldwin

11. 1951

12. Author LeRoi Jones

13. Martin Luther King, Jr.

14. William Wells Brown (**Clotel**, published in 1853)

15. Countee Cullen

16. Charles Fuller

17. Author Frank Yerby

18. Ellen Tarry

19. James Weldon Johnson

20. Chester Himes

21. Poet Langston Hughes

22. Author Jessie Fauset

23. Jupiter Hammon (1761)

24. John Oliver Killens

25. Loften Mitchell

26. Author J. Saunders Redding

27. Joel A. Rogers (1953)

28. New York City

29. Lorraine Hansberry

30. Louis Lautier (1947)

31. **Freedom's Journal**

32. Aaron Douglas

33. Ralph Ellison

34. Alex Haley, Jr.

35. Willard Motley

36. Ntozake Shange

37. Alice Walker

38. Harriet Beecher Stowe

39. Iceberg Slim

40. Bill Russell

41. Donald Gornes

42. **Nigger**

43. James Baldwin

44. Amy Garvey

45. Nikki Giovanni

46. Norman Lear

47. Claude Browne

48. Eldridge Cleaver

49. Stephen Joseph

50. **I Know Why the Caged Bird Sings**

51. Rubin "Hurricane" Carter

52. James Herndon

53. Warren Miller

54. Jonathan Kozol (**Death at an Early Age**)

55. **Negro Digest**

56. **Black Rage**

57. **The North Star**

58. John H. Griffin

59. Richard Wright

60. Jay David

61. Harper Lee

62. Paula Marshall

63. **Family Ties: The Escape or a Leap to Freedom**

64. Nancy Larrick

65. Dr. Martin Luther King, Jr.

66. **Keep the Faith, Baby**

67. Phillip Durham and Everett Jones

68. **Off the Court**

69. Ernest Gaines

70. Mary Wilson

71. **The Black Student's Guide to College**

72. Illinois

73. "A Dream Deferred" by Langston Hughes

74. **Cooley High**

75. Harry Edwards

76. **Color Me Brown**

77. Ernest Tidyman

78. Walt Frazier

79. **Oreo**

80. Lerone Bennett, Jr.

81. David Walker

82. Angela Davis

83. Bobby Seale

84. Julius Lester

85. **Gary Coleman: Medical Miracle**

86. **Ebony Junior**

87. **Uncle Tom's Cabin**

88. **Gnawing at My Soul**

89. **For Colored Girls Who Have Considered Suicide — When the Rainbow is Enuf**

90. Dr. Carter G. Woodson

91. William Edward Burghardt

PERSONALITIES

1. Stepin Fetchit

2. Thelma

3. Ethel Waters

4. Raymond St. Jacques

5. Gordon Parks

6. Melvin Van Peebles

7. Thomas Wright Waller

8. "The Fly"

9. Jones

10. Diana Ross, Florence Ballard and Mary Wilson

11. Steveland Morris

12. Merald Knight, William Guest and Edward Patten

13. Richard Penniman

14. Leroy

15. **Purlie**

16. Pearl Bailey

17. Jackie

18. Bill "Bojangles" Robinson

19. Earl (Fatha) Hines Band

20. George Walker

21. Dinah Washington

22. Marian Anderson

23. Eartha Kitt

24. Sammy Davis, Jr.

25. Antoine Domino

26. Jean Terrell

27. Dean Dixon (1941)

28. Mattiwilda Dobbs

29. Maureen, LaToya and Janet

30. Needlepoint

31. George Lincoln Rockwell (American Nazi Party)

32. Rochester Van Jones (Eddie Anderson)

33. Malcolm Little

34. Jeffrey Holder

35. Kareem Abdul Jabbar and Wilt Chamberlain

36. William

37. Tim Reid ("WKRP in Cincinnati" and the Mutual Black Radio Network—both as "Venus Flytrap")

38. Prince Rogers Nelson

39. Willie Tyler

40. Matt Snell

41. Lou Rawls

42. Slappy White

43. The Golddiggers

44. Jiffy

45. Lawrence Tero

46. Caesars Palace

47. Nipsey Russell

48. At the bottom of a river in Louisville, where he threw it in anger after he was denied service in a restaurant

49. William

50. Aretha Franklin

51. Blues Boy

52. The Harlem Globetrotters

53. Vivian Malone

54. Smokey Robinson

55. Benny Goodman

56. Ferdinand

57. Dr. Carter G. Woodson

58. Walter White

59. Reverend Dr. Ralph David Abernathy

60. Edward Bouchet (1876)

61. Imamu Amiri Baraka

62. Norman Frances

63. Willard Townsend

64. Andrew Brimmer

65. Clerow

66. Dr. Ralph Bunche

67. Ed Bradley

68. Vice Admiral Samuel Gravely, Jr.

69. Dr. William Hinton

70. Benjamin Hooks

71. Private Henry Johnson

72. Elijah Muhammad

73. Eugene Bullard

74. A. Phillip Randolph

75. Carl T. Rowan

76. John Sanford

77. Actress Della Reese

78. Singer Donna Summer

79. "LA Is My Lady"

80. Buck Brown

81. Greyhound

82. Because his mobster buddies thought he was "crazy" to pal around with black people

83. Willie Mays

84. Peggy Lipton of "The Mod Squad"

85. Kim Fields ("The Facts Of Life")

86. John Henry

87. Tavares

88. Domingue Wilkins

89. 7-Up

90. Dingo Boots

91. Love-tron

92. Kareem Abdul Jabbar

93. Alfonso Ribeiro

94. Pele

95. "The Brown Bomber"

POLITICS

1. John Mercer Langston (clerk of Brown-helm Township, Lorain County, Ohio; 1855)

2. 1862

3. The first blacks to be elected to the Massachusetts House of Representatives (1866)

4. Joseph H. Rainey (South Carolina, 1870)

5. Hiram Revels (Mississippi)

6. Illinois

7. Crystal Bird Fauset (Philadelphia, 1938)

8. William L. Dawson (Chairman of the House Committee on Government Operations)

9. John Hyman (1869)

10. They are blacks who have been state representatives.

11. They are blacks who have been state senators

12. 1868 (Andrew Johnson was elected.)

13. Shirley Chisholm

14. Dr. Robert C. Weaver (Department of Housing and Urban Development under Franklin D. Roosevelt, 1941)

15. Ambassadors under the Johnson administration

16. Thurgood Marshall (appointed July 13, 1965 by Lyndon B. Johnson)

17. Edward Brooke (Massachusetts)

18. Dr. Martin Luther King, Jr.

19. The 18th

20. Jimmy Carter

21. All were at one time congressmen from South Carolina.

22. George H. White (North Carolina, 1880)

23. James T. Rapier

24. Josiah Walls (1871)

25. Jefferson Long (1869)

26. Charles Nash

27. Arthur Mitchell (1934)

28. Adam Clayton Powell, Jr.

29. John Conyers, Jr. (Michigan)

30. John Mercer Langston

31. Municipal judge

32. Don Crawford (1965)

33. Conrad Lynn

34. Douglas Dowd

35. Freedom and Peace Party (1968)

36. 1962

37. Sadie Alexander

38. Co-chairman

39. Charlotte Hubbard

40. Elizabeth Koontz

41. Constance Motley (1964)

42. Dentist

43. Gary, Indiana

44. George Edwin Taylor

45. Robert Brown

46. Jesse Jackson

47. She was a Texas state senator.

48. Dorothy Bolden

49. Lieutenant governor (of California and Colorado, respectively)

50. Geraldine Ford

51. J. Ernest Wilkins

52. Apartheid

53. Juanita Stout (1959)

54. Robert Weaver

55. Assistant Secretary of the Department of Health, Education and Welfare

56. Julian Bond

57. Eldridge Cleaver

58. Andrew Young

59. Maynard Jackson

60. William H. Hastie (1937)

61. Donald E. McHenry

62. Ernest Morial (1977)

63. Charles Mahoney (1954)

64. Edith Sampson (1950)

65. Daniel James

66. Booker T. Washington

67. North Carolina

68. Walter Washington

69. William Tolbert

70. Frederick Douglass

71. Nigeria

72. Benjamin Hooks

73. Samuel Pierce (Housing and Urban Development)

74. Cleveland

75. Augustus Hawkins (D-California)

76. Wilson Goode

77. Sammy Davis, Jr.

78. Arthur Fletcher

79. Marion Barry

80. Alabama

81. Ken Gibson

82. Edward Kennedy

83. It contained a dollar bill with his image on it, which was actually being used in change machines.

84. Georgia

85. The award the NAACP gives yearly to the black American with the greatest achievement

86. 1931

87. Lyndon B. Johnson

88. Andrew Johnson

89. **The Boston Strangler**

90. Crispus Attucks

91. Thomas Clarkson

92. Warren Harding

FILM

1. Gregory Hines

2. **Divorce Among Friends**

3. **Sergeant Rutledge**

4. Nat King Cole

5. **In the Heat of the Night**

6. **Brothers**

7. **The Bingo Long Traveling All-Stars and Motor Kings**

8. Billy Dee Williams

9. Actor Bernie Casey

10. Yaphet Kotto

11. **Ragtime**

12. Ghostbuster (played by actor Ernie Hudson in the film **Ghostbusters**)

13. Actress Ruby Dee

14. **Rufus Jones For President** (1931)

15. Lena Horne

16. Actor Earle Hyman

17. James Earl Jones

18. **Gone With the Wind**

19. American Negro Theatre (1940)

20. Paul Robeson

21. Actress Ethel Waters

22. **Shuffle Along**

23. **Hearts in Dixie**

24. Paul Robeson

25. **The Little Colonel** and **The Littlest Rebel**

26. **Rainbow on the River** (1936)

27. **Imitation of Life**

28. **It's a Mad, Mad, Mad, Mad World**

29. **Stormy Weather**

30. Mantan Moreland

31. **Lost Boundaries**

32. **A Day at the Races**

33. Husky Miller

34. **Porgy and Bess**

35. **Dr. Strangelove**

36. **100 Rifles**

37. Actress Diana Sands

38. **Putney Swope**

39. John

40. **Super Fly T.N.T.** (1973)

41. **Sounder**

42. Actor Calvin Lockhart

43. **Hurry Sundown**

44. **Runnin' Wild**

45. Louis Gossett, Jr.

46. Lorenzo Tucker

47. **Pinky**

48. Joe Louis

49. Brock Peters

50. Ray Charles

51. **No Way Out**, **The Bedford Incident** and **The Long Ships**

52. Bernie Casey

53. William Marshall

54. **48 Hours**

55. **Pipe Dreams**

56. Richard Roundtree

57. Isabel Sanford

58. **Ben** and **The Wiz**

59. Rosiland Cash

60. **Best Defense**

61. **Footloose** ("Dancing in the Sheets")

62. **The Well**

63. Isaac Hayes

64. **Wattstax**

65. **The Detective**

66. **Doctor Detroit**

67. Scatman Carruthers

68. Goldie

69. "The Taste"

70. Paul Winfield

71. Cleavon Little

72. **Live and Let Die**

73. Lando Calerisian

74. Julius Irving ("Dr. J.")

75. Jamal Wilkes

76. O.J. Simpson

77. Scatman Carruthers

78. James Garner and Louis Gossett, Jr.

79. **The Sting**

80. **Save the Children**

81. **The Scalp Hunters**

82. Moses Gunn

83. "The Master of Disaster" and "The King of Sting"

84. James Earl Jones and Cicely Tyson

85. Julius Harris

86. Geoffrey Cambridge

87. Fred Williamson

88. Dionne Warwick

89. **Three the Hard Way**

90. "Groove with the Genie"

91. **Airplane**

92. Marilyn Horne

93. Dooley Wilson

94. **Mandingo** and **Drum**

95. Pittsburgh Pirates

96. **Fast Break**

97. Judy Pace

98. Sonny Liston

99. **The Adventures of Huckleberry Finn**

TV/RADIO

1. "The Electric Company"

2. Roosevelt Franklin

3. "Calvin and the Colonel"

4. Morgan

5. Ray and Charles (mice); Rosie (snake)

6. "Fat Albert and the Cosby Kids"

7. "Ruby Valentine" (1954)

8. Lillian Randolph

9. Hattie McDaniel

10. The Mariners

11. Leontyne Price

12. Corey, played by Marc Coppage

13. Lola Falana (announcer) and Quincy Jones (orchestra leader)

14. "Steptoe and Son"

15. Leonard Lightfoot

16. Sammy Davis, Jr.

17. Isaac Hayes

18. "Baby, I'm Back"

19. Scoey Mitchell

20. Lillian Randolph and Beah Richards

21. Otis Foster, played by William Elliot

22. "Carter Country"

23. "Fish"

24. "Chico and the Man"

25. "Rowan and Martin's Laugh-In"

26. "Car 54, Where Are You?"

27. James Junior

28. "CPO Sharkey"

29. "Grady"

30. Mark Sanger, played by Don Mitchell

31. Isaac Washington

32. Odessa Cleveland

33. Howard

34. "Maude"

35. Clifton Davis

36. Barney Collier

37. Eugene, played by Jeffrey Jacquet

38. "The Outcasts"

39. "The Partners"

40. Louis Bellson (her husband)

41. "Peyton Place" and Ruby Dee

42. "The Practice" (starring Danny Thomas)

43. "The Bold Ones"

44. Justin Culp, played by Scoey Mitchell

45. **Cooley High**

46. Cleavon Little (Dr. Jerry Noland)

47. Harry

48. Venus Flytrap ("WKRP In Cincinnati")

49. "Boom Boom"

50. Elizabeth

51. "VEGA$"

52. Toby

53. "Solid."

54. "McCloud," "Battlestar Gallactica," "Gallactica 1980," and "You'll Never Get Rich (The Phil Silvers Show)"

55. Oscar Robertson

56. Time-Life Books series on Viet-Nam

57. 12D

58. "Checking In"

59. Adam Wade ("Musical Chairs")

60. "A mind is a terrible thing to waste."

61. Bill Cosby (for "I Spy")

62. "We wish you love, peace and soul."

63. J.J., Thelma and Michael

64. Benson and Saunders

65. CNN

66. Island Hoppers

67. Eartha Kitt

68. Damon Evans and Mike Evans

69. J.J. Jackson

70. Demond Wilson (Oscar) and Ron Glass (Felix)

71. The Ink Spots

72. "That's My Mama"

73. **Blood on the Badge**

74. "Star Trek" (between Captain Kirk and Lieutenant Uhura)

75. Scatman Crothers

76. Lou Lomax (1959)

77. (Nell) Harper and (Addy) Wilson

78. "Sinner Man," by Sarah Dash

79. Donnie Simpson

80. Huggy Bear Brown (played by Antonio Fargas)

81. "Tenspeed and Brown Shoe"

82. Valerie

83. Aaron Spelling Productions ("The Mod Squad")

84. Silas, played by Napoleon Whiting

85. Arnold (Jackson) Drummond

86. Boomer, played by Herb Jefferson, Jr.

87. Louise, played by Amanda Randolph

88. "Tony Brown's Journal" (formally "Black Journal")

89. Freda Payne

90. Johnny Brown

91. Coke and Mean Joe Greene

92. "Captain Kangaroo"

93. Olivia

94. Michael Garrison

95. "Grady"

96. "Miami Vice"

97. "Sing Along With Mitch"

98. Rodney Allen Rippy

99. Jasper

100. James (played by Ivan Dixon)

VINYL

1. "Satchmo"

2. "It's All In the Game"

3. Quincy Jones

4. Roy Hamilton

5. Columbia

6. Aretha Franklin

7. "It's Magic"

8. Pearl Bailey

9. Composer James Bland

10. "Minnie the Moocher"

11. Mahalia Jackson

12. The Supremes

13. "Maybelline"

14. Imperial

15. Phil Phillips (and the Twilights)

16. Hank Ballard and the Midnighters

17. "Tutti Fruitti"

18. Sam Cooke

19. Marie

20. Anita, Ruth, Bonnie and June

21. The Drifters

22. STAX (Volt)

23. Otis Redding

24. Memphis Group

25. "Please Mr. Postman"

26. Mary Wells

27. "Up The Ladder To the Roof"

28. Epic

29. The Miracles

30. Kim Weston

31. Dunhill (ABC Records)

32. T-Neck

33. "Soul Train"

34. The Delfonics

35. Patti and the Emblems

36. Dee Dee Sharpe

37. The Stylistics

38. The Coasters

39. Lloyd Price

40. The Drifters

41. The Shirelles

42. James Brown

43. The Four Tops

44. The Crystals

45. Bessie Smith

46. The Jackson Five

47. Isley Brothers

48. Buddy Holly and the Crickets

49. "The Godfather of Soul"

50. The Jackson Five, Gloria Gaynor and Isaac Hayes

51. Freda Payne

52. "Hey you . . . almost a doctor!"

53. Roger Miller's

54. "Don't You Worry 'Bout a Thing"

55. The Temptations

56. Berry Gordy, Jr.

57. The Four Tops and the Supremes

58. "Groovy Situation"

59. Ramsey Lewis

60. The Miracles

61. Patty LaBelle and the Bluebelles

62. Aretha Franklin

63. The Jimi Hendrix Experience

64. "Dance To the Music"

65. "Sittin' On the Dock Of the Bay" (Otis Redding)

66. The Versatiles

67. "I Loved You For a Long Time"

68. Buddah

69. Bean Esposito

70. Lucille

71. "Got to Get You Into My Life" (Earth, Wind & Fire)

72. "This Will Be"

73. Love Unlimited

74. A Taste Of Honey

75. Maurice White (Earth, Wind & Fire)

76. Stanley Turrentine

77. The Isley Brothers

78. The Nitty Gritty Dirt Band

79. The Five Blind Boys

80. Leroy

81. Shirley Bassey (**Goldfinger/Diamonds Are Forever/Moonraker**)

82. Steve Cropper

83. Natalie Cole

84. "Here Comes the Judge"

85. The Bus Boys

86. James Brown

87. Bella and Bathsheba

88. Eartha Kitt

89. Rare Earth

90. Franklin Ajaye

91. The Five Stairsteps

92. The Temptations

93. Bobby Womack

94. Skillet and Leroy

95. "The Boll Weevil Song"

96. New Edition

97. Donny Hathaway

98. "Outa-Space"

99. Soul Train Scramble Board

100. **Never Give an Inch** or **Sometimes a Great Notion**

SPORTS

1. Montreal Royals

2. "Cyclone" and "Smokey"

3. Eastern Colored League

4. April 30, 1928

5. James Bell

6. The Negro American League (1937)

7. Emmett Ashford (during an American League game between the Cleveland Indians and the Washington Senators on April 23, 1966)

8. Bill Russell (On April 18, 1966, he succeeded Red Auerbach as coach of the Boston Celtics.)

9. Maury Wills

10. Tom Molineaux

11. Henry Armstrong

12. Floyd Patterson

13. Cassius Clay

14. 100-meter run, 200-meter run, and 400-meter relay

15. Charlie Sifford

16. Oliver Lewis in 1875 (The horse's name was Aristides)

17. Dr. Reginald Weir (1948)

18. Wes Unseld

19. Bobby Bonds

20. Ernie Banks

21. #6

22. 755

23. Walter Payton

24. Eugene

25. Rod Carew

26. Jim Marshall

27. "We Are Family" (performed by Sister Sledge)

28. Ken Griffey

29. Bob Hayes

30. Archie Griffin

31. Baseball and NBA basketball

32. Reggie Jackson

33. Jim Rice

34. Lee Elder

35. Wilt Chamberlain

36. Ferguson Jenkins

37. Branch Rickey (signed Jackie Robinson) and Abe Saperstein (founded Harlem Globetrotters)

38. Because it was the number of his boyhood hero, Willie Mays

39. **Bonnie and Clyde** ("Clyde" became Frazier's nickname.)

40. O.J. Simpson and Fred Williamson

41. Art Monk (Washington Redskins)

42. 1975 (Boston Red Sox)

43. Cicero Murphy

44. Elgin Baylor

45. Marlon Briscoe

46. Chicago Bulls and San Antonio Spurs

47. Kansas City Chiefs

48. Connie Hawkins

49. Reggie Smith

50. Charlie Joiner

51. Muhammad Ali

52. Jimmy Connors

53. The Tigers

54. Gayle Sayers

55. Chuck Cooper

56. Willie O'Reed

57. The Bucketeers

58. Darnell Hillman

59. Ron LaFlore (Tigers/Expos)

60. Roy Campanella (1951, 1953 and 1955)

61. Wilt Chamberlain

62. Althea Gibson

63. The Harlem Globetrotters

64. Jack Johnson (1908)

65. Milt Campbell

66. Super Bowl #3, Jets vs. Colts

67. Jesse Owens

68. Oscar Robertson

69. Sugar Ray Robinson

70. Ferdinand Lewis Alcindor, Jr.

71. Director of the first gymnasium at Harvard University (1859)

72. Mildred McDaniels

73. All were players in the Negro Leagues who were inducted into the Baseball Hall of Fame.

74. Elston Howard

75. Jackie Robinson (1962)

76. Ernie Banks (shortstop)

77. Frank Robinson

78. Biddle and Livingstone (1890)

79. Tom Gatewood

80. Johnny Rogers (running back for the University of Nebraska)

81. Southeastern Conference (1960)

82. Henry McDonald (Rochester Jeffersons)

83. Claude Young

84. Ernie Davis (1961)

85. Jim Nance

86. Roosevelt Brown

87. K.C. Jones

88. 1966-1967

89. Tom Payne (1970)

90. Elvin Hayes

91. Charles

92. John Borican

93. Cornelius Johnson in 1936 (He was still a high school student.)

94. He organized the United Association of Professional Golfers.

95. Alfred Johnson

96. Joe Walcott

97. Joe "Sandy" Sadler

98. University of Massachusetts at Amherst

99. Josh Gibson

CURRENT EVENTS

1. **Dream Girls**

2. Colonel Guy S. Bluford

3. "Rainbow Coalition"

4. Kool and the Gang

5. Robert Goodman

6. Reuben V. Anderson (replacing Justice Francis S. Bowling)

7. Harris (Brown pulled a hamstring.)

8. Louis Farrakhan

9. Bernhard Goetz

10. Robin Marks

11. Black women of the world

12. Kansas City (Missouri)

13. John Thompson

14. Joe Theismann

15. Michael Jackson

16. Dallas

17. Suzette Charles

18. Irv Crosse

19. Wayne Williams

20. Because she mentions the American Express Company

21. "Eat It"

22. George Burns

23. Julius Irving ("Dr. J.")

24. **Against All Odds**

25. Muammar Khadaffy

26. A trip to Africa

27. "Mickey D's"

28. "We Are the World"

29. Richard Pryor

30. Burger King

31. Eddie Murphy

32. Suzette Charles

33. Quaker Cereal Company

34. Addis Ababa

35. Clarence Williams III

36. "Ghost Town"

37. Walter Payton

38. Arthur Ashe

39. The Coast Guard

40. Lionel Ritchie

41. Arnold Palmer

42. Gladys Knight and Flip Wilson

43. Dorian Harewood

44. The New Edition

45. Marvelous Marvin Hagler

46. Randall Robinson

47. Jackie Wilson and Marvin Gaye

48. Quincy Jones and New York Met Dwight Gooden

49. Kool and the Gang

50. Philadelphia

51. Whoopi Goldberg

52. Almost every radio station in the US played "We Are the World."

53. Kareem Abdul Jabbar

54. Frank Viola

MISCELLANEOUS

1. "Mulatto"

2. Carmen de Lavallade

3. Alice Dunnigan (1948)

4. Elizabeth D. Koontz

5. Mary Eliza Mahoney

6. Mary Church Terrell

7. Maggie L. Walker (Independent Order of St. Luke, Virginia and West Virginia, 1900)

8. Thelma Houston

9. Bert Williams

10. Timothy Thomas Fortune

11. Bernard Robinson

12. William Rowe

13. Detroit

14. Dashikis

15. Kwanza

16. Marcus Garvey

17. Glynn Turman

18. Oliver Wendell Jones

19. Iceberg Slim

20. Faberge

21. Laff Records

22. "Reggie-vision"

23. Franklin

24. Dr. Martin Luther King, Jr.

25. Because Lincoln was a Republican

26. A handkerchief

27. The maker of "Soul Potato Chips"

28. Willie Stargell and Terry Bradshaw

29. Gloria Spencer (approximately 800 pounds)

30. Notre Dame High

31. Mississippi (over 35%)

32. Frederick Douglass

33. "The Mighty" Truman Wald

34. The Gray Panthers

35. Reggie Jackson

36. Liberation and self-defense

37. A young man

38. Sarah Breedlove Walker

39. "If you're black, you get back."

40. "Jim Crow"

41. Dock Ellis

42. Rocky Johnson

43. The barber shop

44. Slappy White

45. LaWanda Page

46. Black Vulcan

47. Lieutenant Flapp

48. Celebrate in the endzone after a touchdown

49. Washington, DC

50. Irene Cara

51. The Olympic rings

52. The $2 bill (on the back)

53. The krugerand

54. **Say Amen, Somebody**

55. James Monroe (Monrovia)

56. Yoko Ono

57. Spain

58. Zaire

59. The Civil War

60. "Juvenile Jury"

61. Prince

62. Bob Gibson

63. **Black Enterprise**

64. "Equal Opportunity Employer"

65. The Pips (of Gladys Knight and the Pips)

66. "Partners in Crime"

67. Mike Nesmith

68. Civil Rights (1964), then the Voting Rights (1965)

69. Five (fifty songs)

70. Gorilla Monsoon

71. Uganda

72. Yannick Noah

73. Connecticut, Massachusetts and New Hampshire

74. February 1

75. The Red and the Mediterranean

76. ABC

77. "The Powers of Matthew Star"

78. The US and South Africa

79. "I love you."

80. Harold "Happy" Hareston (formerly of the LA Lakers), Eric "Sleepy" Floyd (Golden State Warriors) and Julius "Doctor J" Erving (Philadelphia 76ers)

81. L.C. Greenwood

82. **The World According To Garp** ("Nature Boy") and **My Favorite Year** ("Twilight Time")

83. Jo Jo White and Kareem Abdul Jabbar (who won)

84. "Affirmative Action"

85. "I Get a Kick From Champagne"

86. Barbie

87. Walter Payton

88. George Scott

89. Louis Gossett, Jr.

90. Haiti

91. Zanzibar and Tanganika

92. Vermont (approx. 0.2%)

93. Cassius X

94. Uganda

95. **Muhammed Speaks**

96. Bryant and Greg

97. England

98. James Bland (circa 1878)

99. Papa Doc

100. **Essence**

101. Reggie Theus and Isaiah Thomas

102. Zambia, Zaire and Zimbabwe

103. "Steal" cable programming

104. Twenty million

105. "The Soul Brother's Top 20"

106. Kampala

107. English

PICTURES

1. Harold Washington

2. Chicago

3. **Deal of the Century**, Gregory Hines

4. Edward Brooke

5. Massachusetts

6. **City Heat**

7. **Fame**

8. Three

9. Mayor Tom Bradley

10. Los Angeles

11. 1984 Summer Olympics

12. Cannonball Run II

13. Bill Cosby

14. Fred Williamson

15. I (for the Kansas City Chiefs)

16. Greg Morris

17. Desert Inn

18. Andrew Young

19. Atlanta

20. Teresa Graves

21. "Get Christie Love"

22. Lite Beer from Miller

23. Jim Rice, the Boston Red Sox

24. The Dominoes

25. Roberta Flack

26. Malcolm X

27. He is a minister.

28. Destroy it

29. The United States Military Academy

30. Charley Pride